INVESTIGATING SOCIETY·
an introduction to sociolc

Denis Lawton BA, PhD
Deputy Director of the
University of London Institute of Edu

Second Edition

HODDER AND STOUGHTON
LONDON   SYDNEY   AUCKLAND   TORONTO

Preface

In a modern industrial society with a compulsory education system, there are good reasons for suggesting that everyone should have the opportunity of studying such subjects as mathematics and science, not because they will necessarily need them in their jobs, but because we live in a scientific, technological society and it is not possible to be a fully participating member of this society without a general understanding of scientific and technological issues. For precisely the same reasons, it has become increasingly clear in recent years that everyone should have the opportunity of gaining a basic understanding of the social sciences. More and more schools and colleges are trying to meet this need, and this book is an attempt to provide a straight-forward *introduction* to one important area of social science – sociology.

Sociology is often regarded as a very difficult subject; on the other hand, we all have a great deal of experience of society and a wealth of 'commonsense' ideas about society. In some ways sociology is an extension of common sense, but in other ways it demonstrates the limitations of some kinds of commonsense explanations. Any short introduction is bound to be incomplete, and possibly unbalanced: I have not tried to give a complete or balanced picture of any of the topics introduced; I have concentrated on developing and applying a sociological perspective to a number of important issues. If studying sociology does anything, it should provoke thought; and if some readers are provoked into disagreeing with me and looking for alternative views elsewhere, so much the better – lists of further reading appear at the end of each chapter.

I have tried to avoid difficult terminology and jargon as much as possible, but no one can get far into sociology without using some technical terms – every subject or discipline uses language in a slightly different way. Rather than hold up the flow of the book by defining each technical term the first time it is used, all the sociology terms have been collected together in a *glossary* at the end of the book.

An important part of each chapter will be the section at the end which invites readers to talk, think, or write in a variety of ways about what they have read, including sometimes looking at some examination questions.

Denis Lawton

Preface to Second Edition

The text of this second edition is essentially the same as the first edition except that I have taken the opportunity to remove any inaccuracies which have been pointed out and also to bring the tables up to date. I should like to thank Miss Jacquie Goodall of the University of London Institute of Education Library, who did the research work necessary for up-dating the tables.

Denis Lawton
London
September 1979

The author and publishers would like to thank the following for permission to reproduce copyright material:
Photographs: pages 2, 31 and 86, Keystone Press Agency; pages 30 and 52, Henry Grant; page 85, Fine Fare; pages 117 and 144, Popperfoto; page 154, Mansell Collection.
Charts and tables: page 47, Routledge and Kegan Paul Ltd; pages 102 and 177, the Controller of her Majesty's Stationery Office; pages 99 and 179, Open Book Publishing Ltd.

Contents

1
What is Sociology?

Difficulty of Definition

One of the interesting things about sociology is that no one seems to be absolutely sure what it is or what it is about. Some books will tell you that sociology is 'the study of society', or perhaps 'the scientific study of society',.but even that fairly straight-forward answer leads to difficulties. The first difficulty is that this answer leads to another question, 'So what is society?' A second difficulty is that there is no mention of *people* in the definition, and surely, whatever else sociology is about, it must be about people. Or is it?

It is probably true to say that most sociologists can be divided into two groups: those who see sociology as the study of people in *society*, and those who see sociology as the study of *people* in society. This is not just a clever quibble on words; it shows two fundamentally different views about 'human nature' which have existed for a long time – long before the word 'sociology' was first used in the nineteenth century. But in more recent times there certainly has been a split between those social theorists who emphasise *people* and those who emphasise *society*.

There are those like Marx who seem to be asking the very basic question, 'Why is it that human beings who begin by being naturally co-operative end up by making each other suffer and exploiting each other?' This view of society and of human nature stresses *conflict*, and invites the conclusion that there must be something wrong with society (not with the individuals in society); and for Marx the answer was that what was wrong with society was *capitalism*, and therefore some *action* was called for in order to change that society. This is one version of the 'people-in-society' approach to sociology which is followed by some Marxists and many other non-Marxist sociologists.

On the other hand, there are many sociologists who share with the seventeenth-century philosopher Hobbes an attitude towards human beings which is rather pessimistic and makes them want to ask such

1

questions as, 'Why is it that human beings who are essentially greedy and selfish manage to co-operate so well in a well-ordered society?' This view of human nature and society gives rise to a range of views about the relationship between individuals and society or individuals and the State. Hobbes's own view was that it was essential for individuals to be *controlled* by the power and force of the State in order to prevent chaos; less extreme views see individual human beings necessarily socialised into systems of norms and beliefs. Some sociologists would see society as somehow superhuman, and they would tend to say that individuals who do not conform to the rules of society are deviants, or social misfits, who should be made to conform or be punished. *Social control* is for them a very important sociological concept.

Sociology is therefore concerned with people living together in groups: to give another fairly common textbook definition of sociology, 'the scientific study of *social life*'.

Why the *scientific* study of society or the *scientific* study of social life? Many people have thought about the relation of the individual to society or to the State, but it is only fairly recently (in the last 100 to 150 years) that it would be appropriate to talk of the *scientific* study of society or of social life. Plato and Aristotle, for example, over 2000 years ago had *theories* about individuals and society. Although their ideas were interesting, they were not concerned to put these ideas to the test in a scientific way. In other words, early philosophers indulged in very interesting speculation about people and about society, but did not make any kind of scientific examination of the evidence to support or contradict their ideas.

Modern sociology is different from the writings of the ancient Greek philosophers or the seventeenth-century philosophers in England. Many sociologists have tried to apply *scientific method*, which has clearly shown itself to be a success in physics, chemistry, and biology, to the study of how human beings behave as members of social groups. That sounds fairly straight-forward, perhaps even a little obvious, but in practice it is much more difficult for man to apply scientific methods to himself than to his physical environment.

Let us take some examples to illustrate the difference between the physical sciences and the social sciences.

In the early days of applying scientific method to the study of food – the science of nutrition – a Dr Pekelharing, in 1905, wanted to investigate the *problem* of what would constitute an adequate balanced diet for mice. Dr Pekelharing was thus starting with a fairly general *theory* – the idea that there was such a thing as a balanced diet, i.e. that being well fed was not just a question of getting enough food but involved the right kind of mixture of foods. Pekelharing then devised an *experiment* to test a more specific *hypothesis*, that milk contained something of dietary importance (as well as protein, which people already knew about). The form of the experiment was as follows: Pekelharing fed his mice a diet of casein (milk protein) mixed with egg white, rice flour as carbohydrate, and lard to supply fat, plus some minerals which were also known at the time to be necessary for an animal's nutrition. This constituted what would in 1905 have been regarded as a sufficient and balanced diet (for mice). But, after a few weeks, the mice in this experimental group died. Pekelharing also had a *control group* of mice who were fed exactly the same diet *except* that they had real milk instead of the casein extracted from the milk. These mice in the control group did *not* die.

3

Having collected this *data* (which I have presented in a rather simplified way) and *analysed* it, Pekelharing came to the *conclusion* that milk contained an unknown substance which was necessary for survival. Eventually, after many more experiments, other scientists identified the substance and later coined the term 'vitamin'.

Experiment

1 *Hypothesis* Milk contains something of importance to diet (in addition to protein (casein)).

2 *Experiment*

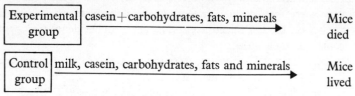

| Experimental group | casein + carbohydrates, fats, minerals —————————▶ | Mice died |
| Control group | milk, casein, carbohydrates, fats and minerals —————————▶ | Mice lived |

3 *Analysis* of data (collected in experiment).

4 *Conclusion* Milk contains another substance (as well as casein) which is necessary for the survival of mice.

This simplified account of a scientific process is also a reasonably good illustration of scientific method in practice. Having made a number of preliminary studies and observations, a scientist works with some general *theory*. In order to test some more specific aspect of that theory, he then develops a *hypothesis*, and an essential thing about an hypothesis is that it should be capable of being tested in some way. In order to test an hypothesis, some kind of *experiment* is needed. The information gathered by means of experiments is called *data*. Data, even in simple experiments, has to be *analysed* so that it can be interpreted by the scientist. Finally, as a result of the experiment, the scientist will come to a conclusion about whether his hypothesis has been proved right or proved wrong, or whether the matter is still inconclusive.

One reason for the difficulty in applying scientific method to human behaviour is obvious: in Pekelharing's experiment some of the mice died. It would be regarded as undesirable for any scientist to experiment on humans if there was even the remote possibility of danger. During the 1939–45 war, some prisoners in concentration camps were, in fact, subjected to dangerous experiments by Nazi doctors; this was universally condemned after the war, and those scientists were charged with war crimes. Occasionally other examples of human beings being

[Source: *Private Eye Cartoon Library 1* (cartoonist, Michael Heath)]

'... in Pekelharing's experiment some of the mice died.'

experimented on come to light, and again those responsible for such experiments are condemned and often punished.

For example, it might be very interesting and valuable for sociologists to select a group of thirty or forty normal new-born babies and have them brought up entirely without adult supervision or intervention (apart from providing them with food and shelter). Sociologists might be interested in this in order to find out what sort of community these children, as they got older, would produce for themselves. Would they develop any kind of language, for example? What tools would they invent? And so on. But it would be unthinkable to run such an experiment, because we believe in the rights of individual human beings. Controlled experiments of this kind are impossible with human beings, and sociologists have to take as their data *not* the findings of experimental research but the information they can pick up from isolated cases of children being abandoned at a very early age. This is much less satisfactory, and much less scientific in some respects – for one thing, the 'evidence' tends to get distorted in the telling and retelling.

Another major difference between scientific procedures in the physical sciences such as physics and chemistry and the human sciences such as sociology and social anthropology is that we also have to take into consideration the fact that it does make a difference when man is studying himself. People react differently when they are being observed, and sociologists can never be quite sure how closely what they are observing approximates to 'normal' behaviour. There is also the difficulty that sociologists have to *interpret* what they see, and this may also be less than 100% reliable. We shall have to return to this point later in the chapter.

Since sociologists cannot usually use human beings in experiments, they have to look at what is happening in non-experimental situations. This is one reason why they often appear to be particularly concerned with *social problems* rather than with normal behaviour. For example, one of the early English social surveys was carried out by a man called Seebohm Rowntree, in 1899. Rowntree was not a sociologist but a social reformer; however, his work is of considerable interest to sociologists, and it has formed the basis of many later sociological enquiries. Rowntree was interested in poverty in York. He found that many working-class families were living in extremely poor conditions: the infant-mortality rate (i.e. the proportion of babies dying within one year of being born) was very high, and he knew that many of those babies were dying from lack of food. One of the interesting ideas that Rowntree developed in this study was his calculation of a 'poverty line'. Families below this line were always under-nourished, but those families with money income above the line would have enough to eat *if* they spent their money wisely. He was able to show that there was a different mortality rate for those families above and below the line, i.e. that poorer people were more likely to die than those who were a bit better off. (Of every 1000 babies below the poverty line, 247 died within their first year; in families above the poverty line, 173 out of every 1000 babies died.)

Table 1
Infant Mortality in York, 1899

	Deaths per 1000 babies
Families *below* the poverty line	247
Families *above* the poverty line	173

This was a very interesting result, and in some ways such data provided arguments which were later to support the idea of the Welfare State in this country. But the term 'poverty' also illustrates another difficulty in social research. What Rowntree drew as a poverty line in 1899 could no longer be regarded as the poverty line in 1936, when Rowntree did another survey of the conditions of working-class families in York. General living standards had improved, so that people who had originally (in 1899) been regarded as above the poverty line were in 1936 well below it. In a neat scientific experiment on animals it is easy to tell a live mouse from a dead one, and so it is easy to come up with clear-cut results. But when we are dealing with human beings, many of our terms, such as 'poverty', are *relative*; that is, we can never define 'poverty' in such a way as that the definition would hold good for ever. Similarly, what would be regarded as poverty in London or Birmingham today might be regarded as comfort or luxury among the peasants of some developing countries.

These are just a few of the many difficulties which exist when we try to look at human behaviour in a scientific way. The difficulties are so great that some people suggest that it is wrong to talk of sociology as being a science at all. The differences between physics, for example, and sociology in the exactitude of observation and measurement make some people prefer not to talk of the 'science' of sociology but of sociology as a '*discipline*'. Others suggest that, although sociology is very different from the physical sciences, there is enough similarity in approach to justify the use of the word 'scientific', even though the methods and procedures are by no means identical with the methods established long ago by the older sciences. We need not go further into the dispute at this stage, but we should consider what it is that makes sociology a discipline, i.e. looking at the world in a way which is different from subjects like physics or biology, or subjects like history. What is the justification for treating sociology as a separate discipline? What is it about sociology which makes us look at the world in a different way?

For sociology to qualify as a discipline, it has to be shown that there are various *generalisations* which can be made about society or about social life, i.e. about people living together in groups; there also have to be certain *procedures* for testing the validity of these generalisations; and finally there have to be certain basic *concepts* and schemes of *classification* which are unique to sociology.

We shall be examining various kinds of generalisation throughout this book, and it will be necessary to use some of the technical terms which sociologists have developed. You will be able to judge for yourselves whether these technical terms and concepts are really useful

7

or whether they simply become jargon which is used to obscure issues rather than to clarify them. Certainly there are a large number of technical terms in sociology, and, as with all such terms, there may be some difficulty in deciding whether a sociologist should invent an entirely new word or should use an everyday word, but use it more precisely and specifically. Exactly the same problem exists in other sciences, of course. In physics, for example, some words have been invented to give a name to something which previously had not been known to exist – such as protons and electrons. On the other hand, physicists also use words which exist in everyday speech, but they use them very differently; for example, 'acceleration' for a physicist simply means a change of velocity, *not* necessarily getting faster. Similarly, in sociology there are examples of invented terms such as *'socialisation'*, but sociologists also use such words as *'class'*, or *'status'*, or *'bureau-cracy'* in ways which are not quite the same as everyday usage but have (we hope) been made more specific. It is very difficult to decide which is the better line for sociologists to adopt: if they invent too many new terms, this tends to cut off sociologists from the rest of the community and makes what they are saying unintelligible to 'the man in the street'; on the other hand, it may be equally confusing for sociologists to use words which the general public *think* they understand but which are in fact being used much more precisely. You may like to look at the following list of fairly common terms in sociology and write down what you think they mean, and then check the results against the glossary which appears at the end of the book.

Social structure	Social class
Social institution	Status
Role	Mobility
Function	Bureaucracy
Kinship	Community
Primary group	Association

Sociology and other Social Sciences

We have seen that sociology differs in important ways from the physical sciences such as chemistry and physics, but in what ways is sociology different from the other social sciences?

The best-known social sciences include *political science, economics, criminology, psychology, demography,* and *anthropology.* In what way is sociology different from these? To some extent, many would argue that the barriers are artificial – they have been established by people working in universities, and the tradition in universities is to have subject departments, and therefore social science has been fragmented or broken up in this way. Certainly sociologists do share with other social sciences a number of generalisations, methods, and specific concepts; but there is one essential difference – sociology is much wider than any of the others. Sociology includes the study of man's political life, man's economic systems, and also studies of crime and delinquency. All of these are considered by sociology and are also considered in a more specialised way by other disciplines. But sociology tries to look at social life as a whole, or society as a whole, rather than to isolate one particular aspect such as the political system or the economic structure. Sociologists are often particularly interested in, for example, the relationship between a political system and an economic structure, and also the relationship of both of these aspects of social life to other parts of society, such as religion and other kinds of behaviour.

Probably the nearest of the other social sciences to sociology is social anthropology, the main difference being that in the past social anthropology was concerned with the study of pre-literate, small-scale communities, whereas sociology has been concerned with modern industrial societies. But this kind of distinction tends to break down for at least two reasons: many pre-literate societies are now 'developing' into industrial or industrialising countries, so the methods and techniques developed by sociologists are in some ways more appropriate than the anthropological ones; on the other hand, some of the techniques developed by social anthropologists, such as participant observation (see below, p. 14), have frequently been employed with good results in modern industrial societies. Many social scientists would argue that the distinction between sociology and social anthropology is particularly artificial and unnecessary; but there are also other kinds of anthropology, particularly physical anthropolgy, which have much more in common with biology than with the social sciences.

Questions for Discussion and/or Written Work

1 Which of the following definitions of sociology do you prefer? Why?
a) The scientific study of society.
b) The study of people in *society*.
c) The study of *people* in society.
d) The scientific study of social life.

2 What are some of the difficulties in regarding sociology as a *science*?

3 In what ways does sociology differ from other social sciences, for example anthropology, psychology, and demography?

4 What do you mean by scientific method?

5 Give some examples of *social problems* that sociologists might study.

Examination Questions

(You will not be able to answer these questions *completely* without further study of later chapters in this book.)

6

a) Describe
   i) what sociology is;
   ii) the kind of research sociologists do;
   iii) what more you now understand about your own society as a result of studying sociology.
b) It has been suggested that scientific method includes the following six processes:
   i) identifying a specific problem;
   ii) selecting appropriate methods to study the problem;
   iii) collecting relevant data;
   iv) analysing the data;
   v) reporting findings and conclusions.

Take any sociological study that you are familiar with, and show how it fits in (or does not fit in) with the six stages quoted above. Make sure that you refer clearly to *one* particular piece of research.

7

28 Die in Syphilis Projects

Washington, September 12

At least 28 black victims of syphilis who were allowed to go untreated in an experiment in Alabama died of the disease, according to a study by doctors involved.

The Public Health Service, under whose auspices the research was conducted, revealed the findings which were first published in the Journal of Chronic Diseases. The experiment, intended to determine through post-mortem what damage untreated syphilis does to the human body, began in 1932 in Tuskagee, Alabama.

The doctors reported that syphilis was established as the primary cause of death in the case of 28 out of 92 patients examined. In the experiment, which involved 600 poor blacks, one-third received no treatment, one-third were treated with arsenic mercury and one-third were free of the disease.

A report on the experiment, published in 1946, said that patients with uncontrolled syphilis suffered hardening of the arteries, abnormal lymph nodes, and loss of vision. – UPI.

[Source: *The Guardian*, 13 September 1972]

Discuss this experiment
a) from a scientific point of view,
b) from a moral point of view (i.e. was it 'right' to conduct an experiment like this?)

Can you think of any other experiments which might be useful but which should never be permitted?

Further Reading

Schofield, M. *Social Research*. Heinemann Educational Books
Worsley, P. (ed.) *Introducing Sociology*. Penguin
Coulson, M. A., and Riddell, D. S. *Approaching Sociology*. Routledge and Kegan Paul
Stacey, M. *Methods of Social Research*. Pergamon
North, P. J. *People in Society*. Longman

2
What do
Sociologists do?

Sociological Method

One essential feature of sociology is the recognition, description, and analysis of *regularities* in human social behaviour. This does *not* mean that individual differences are unimportant but that human behaviour within societies does follow certain observable patterns, even if these patterns vary from one place to another and within one society from one time to another. Part of the sociologists' job is to describe these patterns, to attempt to explain them and to predict social behaviour, even though they realise that *individual* behaviour cannot be predicted. We have seen that sociologists share with the physical scientists a concern for theory and for method of a scientifically valid kind. An over-simplified view of scientific method is to say that the scientist:

1 starts with a theory;
2 derives a specific hypothesis from the theory;
3 makes observations and collects data to test the hypothesis;
4 analyses the data;
5 interprets the data;
6 comes to a conclusion about the hypothesis being confirmed or refuted or remaining in doubt.

This view of science, sometimes called the 'hypothetico-deductive' method, in real life is much more complicated. The scientist (whether he is a physical scientist or a social scientist of some kind) does *not* always start with a complete theory: he can start with an observation or data and derive the hypothesis from that. It would be better to envisage scientific method as a circle or a spiral rather than as a straight line proceeding directly and inevitably from point 1 to point 6.

This hypothetico-deductive model might apply in some ways to the social sciences as well as to the physical sciences, so why is sociology

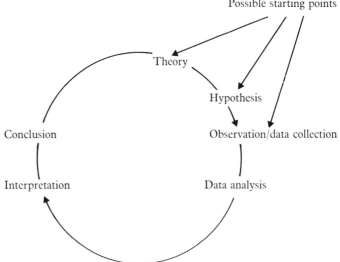

Possible starting points

Theory

Hypothesis

Conclusion

Observation/data collection

Interpretation

Data analysis

different? Clearly the subject matter is different in that it is concerned, as we have seen, with people living in groups, i.e. in society. It may take the form of problem-solving research, as with the example of the Rowntree study of poverty; or it might look at particular institutions in a society, such as the family or education; or sociologists might be concerned to test out much more elaborate theories, such as that class conflict is a fundamental aspect of industrial society. Some sociologists also say that sociology is scientific but is very different from a subject like physics; it is a science, but a human science must have different methods and rules.

When we come to look at a sociologist's sources of data, there are again different kinds to be considered. Sociologists might look at official statistics, historical documents, or contemporary records and documents of various kinds. Or a sociologist might establish his own data by the kinds of survey or observation which we have already looked at briefly. In each case a sociologist has to make judgments about the quality of the data: he should never assume that statistics are correct – errors may have crept into the calculations, or they may even have been deliberately falsified – the same applies to documents, which may have been forged. He also has to be equally careful when he makes his own data, for reasons which will be examined later in this chapter. Sociologists' own data may include the following four kinds:

1 careful observations, systematically recorded;
2 case studies;
3 questionnaires or interviews;
4 surveys (which may involve questionnaires and interviews).

1 Systematic Observation

Much of sociological data is gained by sociologists making careful observations of social situations and social conditions and recording this information in a systematic and careful way – the studies by Seebohm Rowntree, already mentioned, are examples of this kind of work. Alternatively, a sociologist can *participate* in a group or community – this is the method frequently employed by social anthropologists when they want to study a primitive community. A useful distinction to be made is between participant observation of this kind and non-participant observation; for example, much industrial 'work-study' is of the non-participant kind.

One of the most famous examples of participant observation research was W. F. Whyte's *Street Corner Society*. Whyte spent three and a half years as a member of a gang in a Boston slum. He describes the difficulties of being a member of the gang and still being a scientific observer in this way:

'It is well to play a semidetached role: to join in social activities, to bowl, to play ball, to eat and drink together, and so on, but still to have it recognized that you are interested in research. Of course that does not mean interrupting people in the middle of a ball game or a wake for an explanation of the proceedings; it does mean discussing the event thoroughly after it is over. The observer's role must be such that these discussions will be accepted and even welcomed. . . .

They did not expect me to behave just like them. . . . On the other hand, it was extremely important that I accepted with interest everything they did and whatever they said.'

[Source: *Street Corner Society* by W. F. Whyte (University of Chicago Press). Reproduced in *Individual in Society* by D. Krech, R. S. Crutchfield, and E. L. Ballachey (McGraw-Hill)]

2 The Case Study

This method involves an intensive study of one or more subjects which may be used as a basis for generalisation. A case study can be of individuals (e.g. case histories of delinquents or truants from school) or of institutions, such as a school or a prison or a housing area. For example, Jon Rowland, in *Community Decay*, illustrated his analysis of an urban area suffering from all kinds of problems by giving ten case studies of families living in the area. He is not saying that they are a random sample – he has chosen them to *illustrate* (but not to prove) the point that bad living conditions affect *people*.

'Case Five
Family of five.
Living in 3·5 rooms – density of 1·4 p/r.

Very bad housing conditions, damp, no hot water, no bath, no inside toilet. Father always out of work – unskilled. Rent arrears – GLC will not move them or rehouse them. They were rehoused by the council into very bad conditions.
Emotionally psychotic disturbed child – mother apathetic due to conditions. Psychosomatic and physical illnesses. Child mentally subnormal (due to physical environment, lack of stimulation? one of the causes is social conditions).'

[Source: *Community Decay* by J. Rowland (Penguin)]

3 Questionnaires and Structured Interviews

A questionnaire is simply a list of questions which have been prepared very carefully in order to avoid bias or ambiguity. Questionnaires can be given by post, or they can be filled up under the supervision of a sociologist or a research worker. Sometimes it is found even more satisfactory for questions to be read out and the responses recorded either in writing or by tape-recorder. One difficulty of the questionnaire method is that the questionnaire or interview must avoid vagueness but at the same time must be kept simple, and the person being interviewed must usually have only a limited number of alternatives to choose from. But if you give a person only a limited choice you may be 'answering for him', rather than getting at what *he* really thinks or does.

Michael Schofield in *The Sexual Behaviour of Young People* has discussed some of the difficulties involved in using questionnaires *and also in interpreting the results*:

'For example, a number of adolescents thought that the term "birth control" meant controlling the delivery of a baby at birth. Some of the younger adolescents had not heard about venereal disease. When one of the grammar-school boys was asked what he knew about VD he replied: "Nothing, unless you mean vapour density." One of the early questions in the first draft was: "Do you think contraceptives are 100 per cent reliable?" It was hoped that this would indicate a difference in attitude between the experienced and inexperienced boys. Unfortunately the word "contraceptive" was not always understood, and so when the answer was "I don't know", as was usually the case, it was not clear if the answer referred to the reliability of contraceptives, or merely meant that the question has not been understood.'

[Source: *The Sexual Behaviour of Young People* by M. Schofield (Longman)]

4 Large-scale Surveys

The poverty survey in York by Seebohm Rowntree has already been quoted as an example of this kind of research; there have been many others. In your studies of history, you may have read about Chadwick, who in 1842 carried out a survey of sanitary conditions in towns. This involved classifying the population according to social class, and the survey showed that there were different life-expectations for the working class as compared with the middle and upper classes.

Companionship: Do you drink (a) with your wife or (b) because of her?

Tact: Do you tell your wife little white lies (a) for her sake or (b) for yours?

Sharing: Do you give your wife (a) all she deserves or (b) do you restrain yourself?

[Source: *Radio Times*, 19 January 1974 (cartoonist, Bill Tidy)]

'Questionnaires should be kept simple and avoid slanted questions. . . .'

A survey may include every member of a population (like the Census every ten years); more often, *sampling* techniques may be used. Sampling is a way of making general statements about a large number of cases from information derived from only a percentage of the total population. There are two main kinds of sampling:

1 probability or random sampling, and
2 judgment sampling (or quota sampling).

If you want to make a decision about whether apples on a tree are sweet or sour, you do not have to eat all the apples on the tree – a small sample of the fruit will be sufficient. But, even with an apple tree, certain precautions are necessary – you would have to make sure that you were sampling a ripe apple rather than one covered by leaves or one which was less mature than the rest. Similarly, if we want to know the average height of the population of men between twenty-five and forty it would not be necessary to round up all these men and measure them – it would be possible to get very accurate results by taking a sample. We would have to make sure that the sample was a 'good' one, and there are two main methods of making sure that the sample is *representative* and not distorted in some way. We could, for example, take a *random* sample – i.e. one in every 100 or one in every 1000 taken from something like the electoral roll (i.e. not just sending out an interviewer to measure the first 100 men he happens to meet). An alternative method is *judgment sampling*, of which quota sampling is probably the commonest form. Here the technique is to deliberately make a sample *not random* by splitting it up beforehand and saying to the interviewers, 'We want a sample of 1000 men, but they must be drawn from the following occupations in the following numbers, for example, one doctor, three teachers, etc.' In order to prepare a quota of this kind, it would, of course, be necessary to know what percentage the doctors, teachers, etc. are of the total population in the first place.

The surveys based on sampling which are best known to the general public are probably the *public-opinion surveys*. These are sometimes paid for by newspapers to 'find out what the public thinks'. From time to time, surveys are also held (usually of a very small sample) to ask people how they would vote if there were an election. These are meant to test the popularity of the government, or how well the government is dealing with problems of the day. There are all sorts of problems with these opinion polls, but in recent years even hard-headed politicians do not ignore them completely.

Other kinds of surveys based on sampling are used in market re-search. In these days of mass-production of goods, it is important that manufacturers of goods do not produce thousands of a particular kind of car, for example, that no one wants. Market research tries to find out beforehand what kind of things people are likely to want *before* too much expense of design and manufacturing is involved. Market research has to decide not only what people *want* but also what they would pay for it. To help in this, most market-research surveys are a quota sample based on income:

A, B – high-income, professional, and managerial jobs;
C1, C2 – middle range of income, white-collar jobs;
D, E – manual jobs, low income.

Values in Sociology

It is frequently suggested that one of the requirements of being able to regard sociology as a science is that it should be *objective*. This means, for example, that when a sociologist analyses the result of an experiment or any other data available to him he should not allow his own bias or prejudices to influence the way he reports the results. For example, suppose for some purpose I had to find out what percentage of the population was in favour of Britain leaving the Common Market. The obvious way of doing this would be to organise a survey asking a sample of the population what they felt about this; but, since I personally have fairly strong views on the subject, it would be most important for me to avoid letting my own opinion influence the result of the survey. This might happen in a number of ways. When drawing up the questions to be asked in the interview or by a questionnaire, I should have to avoid slanting the line of questioning so that people might be persuaded to answer in a certain way. A 'bad' question might be, 'Do you agree that it would have been better for Britain to remain independent rather than get mixed up with all these foreigners?' Similarly, if I were doing the interviewing myself, there might be a danger of asking even 'good' or 'neutral' questions in such a way as to influence the answers – good interviewers learn not to give nods or grunts or smiles of approval. Finally, when all the results of the survey were analysed, I should have to avoid bias in the interpretation of the results. Suppose, for example, that 51% of my sample were against membership, 40% were for remaining in, and 9% were 'don't knows' – I might be tempted to say 'Most of the population are against staying in the EEC', whereas a fairer conclusion might be, 'Just over half the population are against remaining in the Common Market, compared with 40% who are in favour of remaining.'

At this level, it is quite clear that sociologists have to be on their guard against allowing bias or prejudice to creep into their scientific objective work and their judgments. Peter Berger in his very interesting book *Invitation to Sociology* has suggested that in this respect a good sociologist is rather like a good spy. Just as a spy has to be very careful to report back to his superiors exactly what the true situation is in enemy territory, rather than feed his superiors what they would like to think, so a sociologist has to be very careful to observe what really is happening rather than what he or someone else would like to see happening. This sounds obvious, but there have been many examples of spies who gave bad information, and there have been examples of sociologists who misinterpreted their observations and their data. The possibility of bias influencing professional judgment exists in most professions.

"It's my considered professional opinion, Mrs Stapley, that you need to go on a long sea voyage . . ."

[Source: *Private Eye Cartoon Library 2* (cartoonist, Hector Breeze)]

The possibility of bias influencing professional judgment exists in most professions.

All of this is fairly uncontroversial among sociologists and other social scientists. It does not, of course, mean that sociologists should not have opinions and values; it simply means that sociologists should be very conscious of their values, and should be very careful not to be misled and not to mislead other people. It is also true that a sociologist's values will tend to influence him in the kind of problem that he chooses to investigate. For example, a number of sociologists have investigated various aspects of equality of opportunity in education: they are presumably interested in such problems because they value 'fairness' or social justice (and would like to see more of it in our society). This value need not interfere with objectivity so long as the sociologists do not exaggerate the size of the problem or ignore data which does not fit in with their own opinions. A sociologist or a researcher or a spy does not have to suppress his values, but he must be aware of them. Rowntree presumably chose to look at the question of poverty in York because he felt that something should be done about it, and wanted to collect data to support his argument. This did not mean that his social investigations were of no scientific importance; but, if he had 'cooked the books' to support his campaign, this would have made his work unscientific and worthless.

There is also some disagreement among sociologists about how much they should allow their values to influence them. Some see a sociologist's role as purely descriptive – in the example in the last paragraph about studying inequality of opportunity, some sociologists would see it as sufficient to analyse inequality and its occurrence in education and leave it at that – other sociologists see their work as part of a campaign of *action* to *change* society. That brings us back to the point where this book started, namely that total agreement in sociology is lacking. But there is a great deal on which sociologists do agree, and in this book I will concentrate on what most sociologists would accept, rather than explore too many of the points of disagreement between them.

Questions for Discussion and/or Written Work

1 Under what circumstances might a spy give incorrect information to his superiors? Give some examples – invent them if you wish.

   In what ways might a sociologist misinterpret data and give incorrect information?

2 What do you understand by bias? Give some examples. How can people prevent their own biases from spoiling their judgment?

3 What is the Census? What is it for?

4 If a local council wanted to find out whether the people living in its area would prefer a swimming pool or a sports centre, how could they find out without asking everyone?

5 What is the difference between a random sample and a quota sample?

6

   'In 1963 the Home Office asked the Government Social Survey to interview a sample of youths aged 15–22 to find out something about their ideas on crime and detection. 808 youths were interviewed. One of the many questions they were asked was: "If you committed a crime, which of these things would worry you most about being found out by the police?"'

	% placing item first
1 What my family would think about it	49
2 The chances of losing my job	22
3 Publicity or shame of having to appear in court	12
4 The punishment I might get	10
5 What my girl friend would think	6

6 Whether I should get fair treatment in court   2
7 What my mates would think   1
8 What might happen to me between being found
  out and appearing in court.   2'

[Source: *Crimes, Courts and Figures* by N. Walker (Penguin)]

a) Do any of the above results surprise you at all? Give your reasons.
b) What conclusions would you draw from the results?
c) What *hypothesis* do you think the researchers had in mind?
d) What criticisms would you make of this research? (Remember you
   have seen only a little bit of it.)
e) You *might* find it possible to repeat the survey in your own school
   or college. If so, the results would probably be different. Why?

Further Reading

Douglas, M. (ed.) *Man in Society*. Macdonald. (Especially pages
   329–338 on 'The Work of the Sociologist', but the whole book is
   worth reading and is superbly illustrated.)
Hancock, A. *Survey*. Longman
Central Statistical Office. *Social Trends*. HMSO (annually)
Sillitoe, A. F. *Britain in Figures*. Penguin

3
The Family

If a subject or discipline is worth studying, such as physics or chemistry, we expect it to tell us something of value and interest. What sort of things do sociologists tell us about the family that we did not know already? One of the advantages of sociology is that it makes us look at familiar things in our environment and examine certain features which we tend to take so much for granted that we cease even to be aware of them. Such is the case with the family. Most people have experienced life in a family without thinking what a family means in precise terms, why it exists, or what life would be like without it. On the other hand, many strange statements are made about the family, by journalists for example: perhaps that the family is being destroyed by rising illegitimacy or divorce rates, or by pornography, or even by television. One thing sociologists can do is to clarify the difference between change and destruction, and also between the essential functions of the family and those aspects of family life which are really the frills rather than the basic features. For example, in nineteenth-century English middle-class families it was thought right that fathers should exercise authority and 'protection' over their daughters up to the time of marriage – even if this did not come about until the daughter was thirty. This is much less likely to be true today, but does that mean that, because of this change, the family is somehow less important or influential than it was a hundred years ago? Many would argue that in some respects the family is stronger and more important today, despite such changes.

How Can We Judge?

One way of learning to think more clearly about such words as 'family' is to look further afield. It is a good idea to try to see beyond our own society *now* and to see whether the family exists in all parts of the world, and, if so, what are the differences between the institution of the family in various places and at various times. As a result of such studies we can make some generalisations. All societies have ways of emphasising the physical differences between men and women by the *'roles'* they play in society, especially as regards sexual behaviour, reproduction, and the upbringing of children. All societies have some kind of institution called *'marriage'*, which is really a collection of rules about permanent sexual relations and the duties and obligations of the people involved. It is a mistake, however, to regard marriage as simply a matter of a legal sexual relationship: marriage tends to be connected with all sorts of questions about economic production, the inheritance of property, as well as household organisation of a non-sexual kind. The familiar joke that 'I married her for her cooking' often has more than a grain of truth in it, and there are usually non-sexual advantages for the husband in all societies.

[Source: *Andy Capp* no. 30 by Smythe (IPC)]

So far I have been describing *marriage* rather than the *family*. One of the first things to get clear is that these two institutions are different. In our society, for example, a marriage exists after the wedding, but we could not talk of the married couple as constituting a family. The essence of a family is that two (or more) generations are involved, so we would not talk of the couple's family until a baby was produced (young wives often talk of 'starting a family', meaning to have a baby).

Both husband and wife would normally have been part of their own pre-marriage family (i.e. their parents' family). In order to be quite clear what we are talking about, we might say that the family consists of two elements: marriage and parenthood. (This would not always be true in all societies, but it is certainly true in most societies, including our own, and it is a convenient way of defining the family at this stage.)

This leads us on to another distinction which may be quite useful in our discussion of the family: the difference between a *nuclear* family and an *extended* family. A couple and their child (or children) is a two-generation or nuclear family; an extended family would include the third generation as well – people referred to in our society as grand-parents, uncles and aunts, cousins, etc. It is necessary to say 'in our society', because not all languages divide relatives into the same categories as we do, but all societies do make some kind of distinction between 'family' and 'not-family'.

This difference between the nuclear and the extended family is another source of confusion. Sometimes when people say that the family is declining in importance, they mean the extended family. There is a good deal of evidence to suggest that the nuclear family is *not* declining in our society. When indulging in any serious sociological discussion, it is just as well to be specific about what kind of family we mean, and *'nuclear'* and *'extended'* are useful terms to distinguish whether we mean a couple and their children or whether we mean a much larger family group spread over at least three generations.

If, for the moment, we confine ourselves to a consideration of the nuclear family, it is easy enough to suggest reasons for its existence in human society. The usual explanation – and a very sensible one – is that human babies are very helpless and completely dependent on their mothers for a far longer time than is the case with most other animals. For the first few years, a baby would simply not survive unless he were fed, sheltered, and protected by a mother (or a mother-substitute). But, as well as *physical* survival, when the child is a little older he needs to learn a number of things essential for his *social* survival. His own *language* is largely learned from his mother, and basic *rules* about appropriate and inappropriate behaviour are also learned within the nuclear family. There is also evidence to suggest that human children need love and affection from the person providing food and shelter (usually the mother), and that without this love and affection they do not grow up normally.

Once we get beyond the stage of very basic survival and training for survival, societies vary a great deal in the things that children are expected to learn inside the family and what is learned from the wider society outside the family. In England, for example, children are expected to go to school at the age of five. By that time a child would be expected to 'know how to behave', as well as being toilet-trained and managing to tie his own shoe-laces and blow his nose occasionally. From five years onwards the family hands over to the school a good deal of responsibility for bringing up the child, but not completely – parents are still regarded as being responsible for a good deal of the child's welfare and training. As we shall see in a later chapter, there is some dispute at the moment about the degree of responsibility that a school has, compared with parents, for such delicate matters as moral training and religious instruction.

Not all societies have schools, however, and the division of responsibility between family and non-family training may be very different in those societies; but some kind of distinction will always exist. Just as I pointed out that marriage is not simply a means of legalising sex, so the family is much more than a convenient arrangement for producing and maintaining children (although it is very important for these reasons). Other functions of the family include what some sociologists have referred to as 'placement' and 'socialisation'. Let us consider each of these in some detail.

Placement

Placement essentially means that the family is often partly a means of passing on, or transmitting, certain things from one generation to the next. These things may be property or they may be a status or a social position. For example, in upper-class English families the tradition for centuries has been for the bulk of property to be passed on from father to the *eldest* son (together with a formal title, if there is one). This is a special form of what sociologists call 'patrilineal succession', that is, transmission from father to son. This is perhaps one reason why when women get married they take on the husband's surname, and pass on the husband's surname rather than their own to their children. In societies where property is passed on from mother to daughter (and there are plenty of examples of them), that arrangement is called 'matrilineal succession'. But in England when the Earl of Crumbley dies, his eldest son is 'placed' by acquiring the status or social position of Earl with the title of Lord Crumbley, and all the wealth that goes with it. Younger brothers do not become earls; they acquire a somewhat less exalted 'place' in society, but still a very high one. They will be expected to marry into other noble families and enjoy comfort and prestige ('in a manner to which they have become accustomed').

Similarly, lower down the social scale, where most people do not have any kind of formal title to pass on, we do 'inherit' a social position with certain, possibly limited, expectations and aspirations. Many sociologists claim this to be an advantage even in our society. It would not do, they suggest, if society were a free-for-all with nothing settled in advance, and everyone scrambling for the prizes without any limitations at all. Other sociologists (and my values put me on their side) have their doubts about this in our society *now* (see Chapters 5 to 8). Although we might well agree that in simpler, pre-industrial societies it is 'functional' for the son of a blacksmith to become a blacksmith himself, by a process of 'ascribed status', for a number of reasons such a simple process is not suitable for England today. Whether or not this kind of automatic placement is inevitable or even desirable in all societies, it is certainly true that some kind of placement of the kind described above, that is, for a person's social and occupational future to be predictable to some extent, has existed in societies studied so far. This fact cannot, of course, be used to justify the continued existence of gross inequalties in our own rapidly changing society: to say that something is *right* because it has been going on for a long time is not a convincing argument.

It is certainly true that the young have to be prepared for society, but today the best preparation is not necessarily an acceptance of society as it is now. The preparation might include a willingness to accept change, or even a desire to create change. That brings us on to another function of the family – socialisation.

"You realise of course that they're attempting to condition you into early acceptance of the work principle?"

[Source: *Private Eye Cartoon Library 2* (cartoonist, Hector Breeze)]

Socialisation

'Socialisation' may be defined as the process of learning the ways of a society so as to be able to function within it. There are certain ambiguities in that definition which we will have to leave until later, but it is useful at this stage; and, in any case, this definition of socialisation is much wider than the function of placement described above. I have already mentioned that by the time a child is five and starting school he is expected to know something about appropriate and inappropriate behaviour, which he probably thinks of as 'right' and 'wrong'. He should have learned some, but by no means all, of the rules of his society. Up to the age of five, most of his rule-learning will have taken place within the family; later the other agencies of socialisation, namely *school*, the *peer group*, and *work*, become more important – probably in that order.

But in all societies, including our own, basic or primary socialisation takes place inside the family. In nearly all societies, children learn that roles are different according to sex. For example, girls are expected to play with dolls, but boys are discouraged from doing so. In many societies, children learn that it is not good to interrupt adults who are talking or working; they may or may not learn about respect for other people's property (not all societies share our possessiveness in this way); they will have learned that some people have authority and should be obeyed; they will have learned something about what is regarded as 'right' and 'wrong', including the idea that other people matter – i.e. that it is wrong to be selfish.

All of this is very important – without some kind of rule-system, living in society would be impossible for individuals. How essential the family is to all this is more difficult to establish. What we can say is that so far no completely adequate alternative has been found, although we may need to study carefully the kibbutzim in Israel and the Chinese communes to see how well they work over a fairly long period of time. But even these two institutions do not completely replace the family – they merely reduce its central position of importance. It is certainly true that without some kind of system for passing on 'culture' from one generation to the next we could not survive, and socialisation plays a very important part in this transmission process.

It is also clear that if children up to, say, the age of five experience rules only in the nuclear family, then they may get a limited and inadequate view of the wider social world. It is often for this reason that some people suggest that socialisation is easier or more efficient where the burden is shared not only by members of the nuclear family but by the extended family, so that it is not just the mother and father who bring up children but many other adults as well, together with older children in the nuclear family.

The Individual and Society

We might say, then, that an important reason for the existence of the family is to prepare the child for society. This does not necessarily mean a negative or purely conformist training, and the preparation of the child for society would normally include protecting the child from society; a related function may of course be to protect society from the child – any untrained animal is potentially dangerous, or at least a nuisance, and this includes the human animal as well. For these reasons the family can be said to be 'functional' or to serve a function of mediating between the individual and society. Every society has an extremely complicated culture which the growing child has to learn about; in no society is it possible for a child to grow up and fit in 'naturally'. The essence of culture is that things are passed on from one generation to the next which are not 'natural' and which the child cannot therefore be expected to understand without preparation: he needs to learn about them or be instructed in some way. For example, a child's developing mind is *not* like a camera taking exact photographs of the world: perception and understanding depend on some kind of selection being made, and every society makes certain different kinds of selection. One function of the family is to help to define the world for the growing child: to see what is important, what is less important; what is forbidden, what is accessible; what is good, what is bad. A related function is for the family to help the child to develop some notion of 'self'. Human beings are the only animals possessing this notion of self or identity.

Some sociologists regard the development of self as the growth of understanding of the collection of roles that an individual has to play in society. Once again this is something which begins in the family. The child learns that he is playing the role of child, which is different from the role of parent; that the role of brother is different from the role of son or the role of cousin, and so on. In other words, life in every human society is so very complicated that we have to begin by easy stages, and the family serves the purpose of bringing about a basic understanding of the basic rules and roles before the child is exposed to the much more complicated, and possibly harsher, wider society.

The Changing Family in England and Wales

Many people, making comparisons between the family now and some kind of picture they have (possibly a false one) of the Victorian family, suggest that we are getting worse in some ways. Let us try to assemble some of the *facts* about the family then (say a hundred years ago) and now.

Size of Family

One fact we can be very sure about is that in England during the last hundred years the average number of children in families has fallen, and fallen fairly dramatically. The average Victorian married couple produced about six children, compared with an average of between two and three children today.

Table 2
Changes in the Distribution of Family Size

Number of children born	Marriages taking place about 1860, England and Wales[1] %	Marriages of 1925, Great Britain[2] %	Marriages of 1951, England and Wales[3] %	Marriages of 1965, England and Wales[4] %
0	9	17	13	10
1	5	25	23	18
2	6	25	30	49
3	8	14	17	18
4	9	8	17	5
5	10	5	Over 4	
6	10	3		
7	10	2		
8	9	1		
9	9	0·6		
10	6	0·4		
Over 10	10	0·3		

[1] Figures based on 1911 Fertility Census
[2] Figures taken from 1946 Census
[3] First marriages of all women aged under 45 at marriage, after 21 years marriage
[4] First marriages of all women aged 20–24 at marriage, after 10 years marriage
[Source: *Report of the Royal Commission on Population 1949* (HMSO), *The Current Tempo of Fertility in England and Wales*, by S. M. Farid PhD for the Office of Population Censuses and Surveys, 1974 (HMSO) and *Population Projections 1976–2016*, 1978 (HMSO)]

Table 3
Family Size: Mean Ultimate Family Size for Completed Families

	Year of Marriage	Family Size
Actual	1861–69	6·16
	1900–09	3·30
	1920–24	2·38
	1925–29	2·17
	1930–34	2·13
	1935–39	2·07
	1940–44	2·09
	1945–49	2·22
	1950–54	2·30
	1955–59	2·38
Estimated	1961	2·43
	1971	2·39
	1981	2·41

[Source: *People in Society*, by P. J. North (Longman), compiled from *Registrar General's Statistical Review 1968*, *Social Trends* no. 2, 1971 and *Population Projections 1970–2010* (HMSO), and *Social Trends* no. 8, 1977 (HMSO)]

Many writers have assumed that the modern small family is somehow odd or even unnatural, but before we accept this view we ought to be

sure about whether the Victorian family was not, for some reason, different from the typical pattern of previous centuries. Recent studies by social historians, such as Peter Laslett in *The World We Have Lost*, have collected data from parish registers and other documents to show that, although more children were born per family in the pre-Victorian ages than is usual today, many more of them died in early childhood. So in the seventeenth century the number of children who survived into late childhood and adult life was probably not very different from the present number. The Victorian large family cannot be explained entirely by more children being born; the really significant factor was that more survived, because of better sanitation and medicine. It was

not until the 1870's that the number of children born per married couple gradually began to decline. At first this kind of family limitation was confined to the upper-middle-class families, then the trend began to work its way down the ranks of the lower middle classes, until during the twentieth century the working classes were also successfully limiting the size of their families. Even today there is a social class difference in size of family, but this is much less marked than it was, even in 1951.

Table 4
Fertility According to Social Class, GB

Social Class	No. of children	
	1951[1]	1971[2]
1. Professional etc. occupations	1·88	2·26
2. Intermediate occupations	2·00	2·18
3N. Skilled non-manual occupations ⎱	2·36	2·02
3M. Skilled manual occupations ⎰		2·37
4. Partly-skilled occupations	2·78	2·40
5. Unskilled occupations	3·18	2·74
All	2·44	2·33

([1] Average no. of legitimate live-born children to women aged 20–24 at marriage, married only once, whose marriages had lasted for 20–24 years.
[2] Average no. of live-born children to women in first marriage at 1971 census, whose marriages had lasted for 15–19 years.)

[Source: A Survey of *Social Conditions in England and Wales as illustrated by statistics* by A. M. Carr-Saunders, D. Caradog-Jones, and C. A. Moser, © 1958 Oxford University Press (by permission of The Clarendon Press, Oxford), and *Demographic Review 1977* (HMSO)]

Parent/Child Relationships

Another way in which we can be fairly sure that important changes have taken place is in the way that children are treated by their parents – the whole question of parent/child relationships.

Clearly it is more difficult to measure changes in attitudes and relationships than it is to work out the average family size from what are sometimes called 'hard data' derived from very reliable sources such as the Census figures, or figures worked out from registration of births and deaths etc. But even so, we can be reasonably confident from studies of memoirs, diaries, and autobiographies, as well as more 'objective' descriptions of family life, that the way parents treated their children and expected them to behave was very different in 1870 from what we regard as 'normal' today. In the nineteenth century, the 'normal' attitude of parents to children was one of giving commands and expecting obedience and submission. To some extent this may have been the result of size – it is much easier to be 'democratic' and discuss reasons where numbers are small – but adults also generally felt that it was right that they should give orders and that children should obey without question. Children tended to be treated not as individuals with unique personalities but as an inferior group who should always do as they were told. Father especially tended to be aloof and remote – it was not generally regarded as a father's job to play with children or to read them stories. A mother was expected to instruct children, unless she was rich enough to afford a nanny, in which case the relationship between mother and child might also be very remote. Children were dealt with 'strictly', punished harshly for disobedience, and were not thought to need even the same kind of food and comfort as adults. Children of the 'lower orders' would also very probably have been working long hours under very unpleasant conditions during the first part of the nineteenth century, and this attitude to children persisted even after child labour in factories ceased to be legal. The idea of children needing to play would have been very surprising to most Victorian parents.

This kind of attitude to children has gradually been replaced by one which is sometimes called 'child-centred'; that is, one in which the child is regarded as an individual whose feelings have to be taken into account – to some extent at least. Today, children tend to share in adult life to a much greater extent. Parents play with their children, and the family as a unit spends a great deal of leisure time together; children often join in all sorts of discussions, such as where to go for a holiday, or how to spend time on Saturday afternoon.

One of the dangers of some acquaintance with sociology is the tendency to over-generalise, that is, to assume that what is or was a fairly *typical pattern* was completely or nearly universal. There were certainly Victorian families which did not fit into this typical pattern described above, and there are still plenty of families today which retain many of the characteristics of Victorian families. As well as this, it is very important to remember when we talk of 'typical' family life that there are probably important social-class and regional differences in our society today. There is a great deal of evidence to suggest that working-class parents are more 'indulgent' or easy-going than middle-class parents. The work of John and Elizabeth Newson, for example, has shown that working-class parents are more likely to allow their children dummies, and are less strict about bed-time and toilet training than are middle-class parents. On the other hand, working-class mothers are more likely to punish children physically, and are less tolerant about genital play. In other respects, middle-class mothers expect a high standard of self-control and are less likely to put up with temper tantrums, or physical violence.

I shall return to the importance of social-class differences in a later chapter, but it is very important when discussing changes in family life not to make statements which are too sweeping about changes which have taken place. As a *generalisation* it is certainly true that attitudes to children have changed over the last century and that most parents are probably much closer to their children now than a hundred years ago. But we should always qualify such generalisations as much as possible. We cannot get far in sociology without making generalisations, but studying sociology should also teach us not to confuse a general statement with specific examples.

It is also important not to fall into the trap of regarding ourselves as the 'goodies' and the Victorians as the 'baddies'. There are certainly advantages in the modern close-knit nuclear family structure, but there are disadvantages as well: there is a danger of children in small families being spoilt or over-protected; there is a great danger of parents being *too much* involved in their children's lives – so much so that some psychologists, such as R. D. Laing, have condemned the modern family structure as psychologically dangerous and restricting children's development:

'Some families live in perpetual anxiety of what, to them, is an external persecuting world. The members of the family live in a family ghetto, as it were. This is one basis for so-called maternal over-protection. It is not "over" protection from the mother's point of view, nor, indeed, often from the point of view of other members of the family.'

[Source: *The Politics of Experience* by R. D. Laing (Penguin)]

From a very different point of view, the social anthropologist Edmund Leach also criticises the modern family and points out some of the advantages of older patterns of family life:

'In the past, kinsfolk and neighbours gave the individual continuous moral support throughout his life. Today the domestic household is isolated. The family looks inwards upon itself; there is an intensification of emotional stress between husband and wife, and parents and children. The strain is greater than most of us can bear. Far from being the basis of the good society, the family, with its narrow privacy and tawdry secrets, is the source of all our discontents.'

[Source: *A Runaway World?* by E. Leach (BBC Publications)]

Others have also condemned the modern small family as being too 'inward-looking' and as encouraging a narrow selfish attitude rather than a genuine social one.

Changing Roles of Men and Women in the Family

To some extent the changing role of men and women in the family is connected with changing attitudes of parents and children considered above. One of the factors involved in these changes is the increase in concern for social justice or 'fairness' in society. This can be seen in various ways when studying nineteenth century England: parliamentary reform or the idea of fairness in being represented in government; religious tolerance; greater 'equality between the sexes' (emancipation of women); and a generally greater regard for the rights of individuals – including the rights of women and children.

So in the nineteenth century a woman was more likely to be regarded as her husband's property than as his partner or companion, sharing his duties and responsibilities and providing mutual affection and support on equal terms.

As a generalisation, it is true that there have been important changes in husband/wife relations, but once again we must avoid exaggerating the trend and regarding the change as a total one when it is by no means complete or universal (hence the growth of 'women's lib'). It is also important to stress once again the continued existence of regional and social-class differences. For example, in those areas where the work situation is still of a dangerous kind which emphasises team-work and toughness, there may well be a tendency for women to continue to occupy an inferior social position. The two best examples are perhaps coal-mining and deep-sea fishing. In both of these examples the work is dangerous and demands a great deal of co-operation between men. At the coal face or on a trawler, a single mistake could cause a serious accident resulting in the death or serious injury of a workman. It has been suggested that men have a mixed attitude to this kind of work: they see it as manly work which pays well, but they also feel themselves to be very much at the mercy of the elements – more like a piece of machinery than an individual. When off duty, they may want to forget their work, and a common way of doing this is to drink a great deal when money is available. Another tendency is to use their leisure time drinking in the company of their work-mates rather than their wives, who have no understanding of what they are escaping from. The role expected of a wife is that she will comfort her husband and nurse him, but will not share her troubles with him. In one account of a coal-mining community (*Coal is Our Life* by N. Dennis, F.Henriques, and C. Slaughter), a wife told one of the sociologists writing the book how she went to the cinema and asked her sister to prepare a meal for her collier husband when he came back from the mine. When the husband returned, he threw his dinner to the back of the fire – not because it was not to his taste but because it was his wife's duty to provide him with meals and she had no right to bring in a substitute cook. This role of a wife is very different, therefore, from that of a wife in a middle-class suburb, especially one working herself. Similarly, Jeremy Tunstall in *The Fishermen*, about the Hull trawlermen, said that some men regard their wives simply as inferior providers of sexual and cooking services in return for a weekly wage:

'While he is at sea the fisherman arranges for a regular weekly amount to be sent to his wife. The man can choose any amount he likes but any fisherman who allots his wife less than the whole of his basic wage is likely to become an object of derision to his mates ...

The fishermen themselves are invariably against their wives working. When ashore, a fisherman likes to have all his meals cooked by his wife, and since his turn-round time between trips is more often than not in the middle of the week, this alone prevents his wife going out to work. But even in the fish processing houses, which are often willing to let women come and go very casually, and would not object to a woman taking three days off every three weeks, few fishermen's wives are found at work. Fishermen often think it is an insult to their capacity, or perhaps to their status as men, if their wives go out to work. What is the point of his sacrifice, his willingness to go fishing and to accept its hardships in order to get money, if his wife then decides to go out to work as well? Fishermen say quite frankly they are jealous of their wives going out and meeting men – which would of course happen at work. Similarly most fishermen while at sea discourage their wives from going out in the evenings. They are often critical too of the extent to which their wives visit their own mothers. But they accept mothers-in-law at worst as a necessary evil.

Among fishermen a rough agreement exists as to what is reasonable behaviour for a fisherman in his marriage. It is widely believed that during a turn-round time of three days between trips, a man should spend some time with his wife apart from eating and sleeping with her. On the other hand it is regarded as unusual for a fisherman to spend all three evenings with his wife. Men who only go out drinking when accompanied by their wives tend to regard themselves as unusually virtuous.'

[Source: *The Fishermen* by J. Tunstall (MacGibbon and Kee)]

Once again we should avoid making sweeping over-generalisations about all miners' families or all the wives of deep-sea fishermen – the evidence we have is concerned with a general picture, and we can be sure that there are many exceptions to the general pattern. Nevertheless, there are important differences in some parts of the country and in some occupational groups in what would be regarded as a 'good' family life. But, even in these 'traditional' areas, the pattern may be changing gradually, and Tunstall also points out that in recent years the divorce rate among Hull fishermen has been about twice as high as for other working men in the same area.

The Changing Role of Women

The position of women inside the family is very probably connected to some extent with changes in society as a whole. Married women can now combine a career with a family life, since on average they spend less of their lives pregnant, feeding, or bringing up their young children. Professor Richard Titmuss has estimated that in 1890 the typical working-class mother would marry in her teens or early twenties and would become pregnant ten times. She would spend *fifteen years* of her life 'tied to the wheel of child-bearing'. Today the equivalent time for the average mother is only *four years*. Titmuss rightly calls this a *revolutionary* enlargement of freedom.

On the other hand, we should not under-estimate the other kinds of emancipation which have affected family life. At the beginning of the nineteenth century, for example, a married woman had no right to vote and no right to property. After marriage, all her possessions became legally the property of her husband; even her own children were also legally the husband's in the case of any dispute. Gradually, changes took place both in public opinion and in law, so that husbands were, for example, deprived of their legal right to beat their wives.

Women were also provided with greater educational opportunities (although even today complete equality is lacking), as well as political equality. What effect did this emancipation have on family life and relationships within the family? As we have seen, today it is much more likely (but by no means certain) that a husband and wife will be equal partners in a marriage, sharing duties and responsibilities even to the point of fathers changing nappies, pushing prams, and doing the washing-up. In this sense, we might say that the typical twentieth-century family is more democratic and less autocratic. The fact that a wife works may also have some effect on husband and wife relations: it is often said that a woman who earns money herself is more independent financially and therefore more independent mentally. This may be true to some extent but we should not forget that in many working-class areas in the past it has been *normal* for women to work without this automatically granting wives an equal status.

Working Mothers and Their Children

Another popular belief which sociologists look at sceptically is the often expressed view that 'working mothers neglect their children'. Magistrates, and even social workers, have sometimes used this argument and bemoaned the plight of 'latch-key' children who become juvenile delinquents or maladjusted. But what is the evidence? Is it really true that the married woman's place should be in the home? One study (by Yudkin and Holme, in 1965) analysed the home situations of 300 women working in a Bermondsey biscuit factory. The enquiry found that the women worked not only for additional money but also for companionship. The money they earned tended to be spent on refurnishing or redecorating their houses, also on clothes, toys, and holidays for their children. In most cases, the mother arranged her working hours to fit family responsibilities; there was no evidence at all of neglect of children – any clash of interests was resolved by the mother staying at home. This was, of course, a study of *only one* factory, and so we cannot draw conclusive generalisations about *all* working mothers on this evidence. But there have been a number of other studies and *none* of them have supported the view that any harm is caused to children *of school age* when their mothers go out to work. Some studies have specifically looked at the difference between children of working and non-working mothers as regards delinquency and maladjustment. There were no striking differences in any of these studies and, if anything, the children of working mothers appeared to be more independent, to be healthier, to be better attenders at school, to score more highly in school-attainment tests, and to show fewer signs of maladjustment. One particularly interesting study divided women into three groups: non-working mothers, mothers who worked spasmodically, and regular workers. The result was that there was no difference found between the regular workers and the non-workers, but those mothers who worked on and off tended to have children with problems of some kind.

It is at this point that we meet difficulties of interpretation. One possibile conclusion might be that it was not working or non-working which caused the trouble but the irregularity of the routine. However, another kind of interpretation would deny any necessary connection between work and the existence of maladjustment. This would suggest that mothers who do not or cannot keep a job might also tend to be unstable, unsatisfactory mothers. This conclusion would suggest that there may be good and bad mothers who work and other good and bad mothers who stay at home. We have no evidence that a bad mother who works would improve as a mother if she stayed at home all day, and there is certainly no evidence to suggest that a good mother who stays at home would be any less good if she went to work.

I stressed that this evidence applied mainly to children of school age, and possibly to children of nursery-school age, that is, at least three-years old. Psychologists are fairly certain that in the first three years of life a child needs a mother or an adequate permanent mother substitute. While the child is learning early bodily and social skills – especially language – it appears to help if the child has just one person to guide him through. There is evidence to show that, at this age, children who are deprived of their mothers for any length of time grow up to be rather more demanding and dependent than would be regarded as normal. They tend to insist on a share of the mother's attention long after they would normally have become more outward-looking and independent.

But we also have to remember that some women in our society are really compelled to go out to work even when their children are very young, for example, widows, wives whose husbands have deserted them, and unmarried mothers. At the beginning of this century only about 25% of working women were married; in 1960 more than 50% of the female labour force was married (about 4 million). The fact that more women are getting married is one reason for this increase, but women are also tending to get married at an earlier age. So the typical working woman in 1900 was a young unmarried girl filling in the time while looking for a husband; the typical working woman today is married and approaching middle age. But it is important to remember that working-class women have always worked – in pre-industrial England in the fields, or at home spinning and weaving. In industrial England women were the factory labour force in many trades – for extremely long hours in deplorable conditions. Today at least they work in better physical conditions and for a limited number of hours.

Questions for Discussion and/or Written Work

1 What effect might the availability of the contraceptive pill have on (a) marriage, (b) the family? Why?

Marriage

Great Britain

	1901	1911	1921	1931	1951	1961	1966	1967	1968
Marriages									
Total (thousands)	291	307	360	344	402	387	426	428	452
Spinster marriages									
Proportions per thousand by age:									
16–19	84	76	92	101	168	284	326	301	290
20–24	476	471	478	472	532	512	515	545	562
25–29	278	299	276	283	179	117	93	91	91
30 and over	162	154	154	144	121	87	66	63	57
All ages	1000	1000	1000	1000	1000	1000	1000	1000	1000
Total spinster marriages (thousands)	268	286	326	326	358	350	382	382	402
Average age of spinsters marrying (years)	*25·6*	*25·6*	*25·5*	*25·5*	*24·6*	*23·3*	*22·7*	*22·7*	*22·7*
Bachelor marriages									
Proportions per thousand by age:									
16–19	16	16	21	20	28	70	102	97	93
20–24	404	375	380	365	456	528	563	584	600
25–29	350	380	356	405	318	256	218	208	203
30 and over	230	229	243	210	198	146	117	111	104
All ages	1000	1000	1000	1000	1000	1000	1000	1000	1000
Total bachelor marriages (thousands)	261	280	327	317	349	347	378	378	398
Average age of bachelors marrying (years)	*27·2*	*27·3*	*27·6*	*27·4*	*26·8*	*25·6*	*24·9*	*24·8*	*24·7*
Female population: marital status									
Percentage of females in each age-group who were ever married:									
20–24	—	24·0	27·0	25·5	47·3	57·4	58·2	57·1	57·1
25–29	—	55·8	58·2	58·4	77·5	84·3	85·5	85·7	85·7
40–44	—	81·6	81·6	81·4	85·3	90·1	91·3	91·5	91·7
Live births									
Illegitimate as percentage of all live births	4·2	4·7	4·9	4·8	4·9	5·8	7·7	8·2	8·4
Percentage of legitimate live births within eight months of marriage by age of mother:									
under 20	—	—	—	—	55·0[1]	56·5	54·9	56·4	58·4
20–24	—	—	—	—	12·2[1]	10·5	10·7	11·8	12·1

[1] England and Wales maternities only.

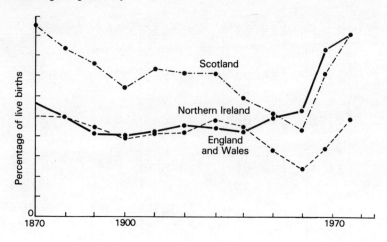

Illegitimate Birth Rate: U.K.
[Source: *Britain in Figures* by A. F. Sillitoe (Penguin) and *Facts in Focus* 1978 (HMSO)]

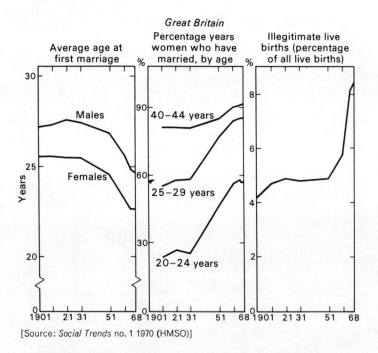

[Source: *Social Trends* no. 1 1970 (HMSO)]

a) What does the table on page 39 tell us about the average age of people getting married?
b) Is marriage getting more or less popular?
c) What do you notice about the illegitimacy rate?

40

d) Do any of these figures surprise you? Why?
e) Does this table support the view that the family is declining in importance? Give your reasons.

3

Table 5
Size of completed family of manual and non-manual workers according to date of marriage.

Date of marriage	Average number of children Non-manual workers	Manual workers
1900–09	2·79	3·94
1910–14	2·34	3·35
1915–19	2·05	2·91
1920–24	1·89	2·72
1927–31	2·08	2·77
1952–56	2·15	2·50

[Source: figures for 1900–1924 taken from the *Report of the Royal Commission on Population, 1949* (HMSO); later figures estimated from the *Demographic Review 1977* (HMSO)]

a) Comment on the 'pattern' you see in the above table.
b) How would you account for the changes between 1900 and 1956?
c) How would you explain the class difference in size of family?
d) Does the table tell us anything about the *quality* of family life?

4

Is the Family Dead?
By Dr Eustace Chesser

The biological purpose of the family is to rear children. If there are no children of a union I do not think we can properly call it a family.

A surprising number of distinguished churchmen, sociologists and psychologists have given various reasons for holding the belief that the family as an institution is dying.

There is nothing very new in this idea. Friedrich Engels and Karl Marx were convinced that the bourgeois family was based on private property and would disappear when capitalism was replaced by socialism. The Bolsheviks took this seriously after 1917 and did their best to make it true. Registration of marriage ceased to be obligatory, abortions were free and legal, it was easier to get a divorce than to buy a pair of shoes, and the traditional taboos were abolished. In less than 20 years, however, all this was reversed, and the family has now emerged stronger than ever.

Opponents of the family unit may well retort that the Russian experience supports their claim that the family is part of an authoritarian structure. The point was recently made by Dr David Cooper that the family is an instrument of indoctrination. In a less extreme form, Dr Edmund Leach has argued that in our society parents and children take too much out of each other. 'The parents fight; the children rebel. Children need to grow up in larger, more relaxed domestic groups centred on the community, rather than on mother's kitchen – something like an Israeli kibbutz, perhaps, or a Chinese commune.'

In the majority of kibbutzim, children are looked after communally from birth, but a close relationship between parent and child is maintained. The fact that the parents are not the disciplinarians saves the children from the resentments and ambivalence we find in other systems.

It appears that very young children show some of the signs which would be attributed in our society to maternal deprivation – e.g. thumb sucking, tantrums, uncontrolled aggression. But by the age of 10 or 11 these symptoms of emotional disturbance tend to become less evident. The children have a relatively smooth adolescence and mostly turn into stable, sociable extroverts.

The system suggests that at least in special circumstances there can be a successful alternative to the traditional form of the family. We must remember, however, that the background of a kibbutz is vastly different from that existing in our urban community.

Today the state provides pre-natal attention, medical and nutritional care from birth, compulsory schooling – with transport in many cases – then grants for higher education. At co-educational schools in Sweden boys as well as girls are taught the elements of childcare. Men are not only expected to do their share of the housework, but to undertake some of the chores long thought to belong to women.

Undoubtedly the authority of the modern father has been undermined, partly at least by the role of the state. Rebellion against all kinds of authority has been carried to lengths that would have been incredible not long ago. The Old Left – Marxism – has come to terms with the family, but the New Left, with its doctrine of continuous revolution against all authority would like to see the family disintegrate.

Few, if any, wish to return to the heavy paternalism of Victorian days. But there is good evidence that the healthy development of children requires a father as well as a mother. And children who really defy 'the system' (instead of just talking about it) – the delinquents and vandals – nearly always come from disturbed families.

More than 50 years of psychological medicine have made it abundantly clear that the seeds of a variety of personality disorders are to be found in early childhood. When all allowance is made for exaggeration it has been established that there is a correlation between the early child–parent relationship and a whole range of problems from delinquency and aggression, to various forms of impotence.

It would be surprising if this were not the case. The influence of parents, brought to bear at the most impressionable period of a child's life, is bound to be far-reaching. This is what gives the family its tremendous significance. Love is as necessary as food. The child needs to feel safe in a dangerous world, and the loving care of those in charge of him brings this sense of security. Without it he must try all sorts of psychological defences.

Even those who believe that the family is a legacy of the bad old days, must admit that until some alternative is found, the breakdown of family life may have a traumatic effect on children. And what alternatives are there?

Children are either brought up in a home, or in an institution. The home need not be that of the real parents. A very young child cannot distinguish a foster-mother from his real mother. But he cannot bring himself up alone. The style of family life has changed throughout the centuries and is now in the process of adaptation to the conditions of the second Industrial Revolution. But the core of the family – father, mother and child – remains constant. The fact that many mothers now have regular employment does not threaten the emotional relationship, and I do not fear that we are approaching a brave new world in which marriage is unnecessary and skilled eugenists impregnate women from suitable stock in a semen bank.

The majority of people have an old-fashioned affection for their children. They are better fed and better educated than ever before. They in turn will evolve a pattern of family life suitable to the conditions they find, with greater freedom and less hypocrisy. If the state makes this easier we need not fear that the family is in decline.

Dr Eustace Chesser is a consultant psychiatrist and has written over 30 books on sex and sociology.

[Source: *The Daily Telegraph Magazine*, 24 September 1971]

a) What does Dr Chesser suggest about the advantages and disadvantages of children being brought up in a kibbutz?
b) Dr Chesser argues that the authority of the modern father has been undermined. Do you think he proves his point by the evidence he quotes?
c) What does Dr Chesser suggest about the future of the family? Do you agree?
d) Comment on any other points in the passage you find interesting or surprising.

Further Reading

Douglas, M. (ed.) *Man in Society*. Macdonald. (Chapter 5, 'Family Kinship and Marriage')
Butterworth, E. and Weir, D. (eds) *The Sociology of Modern Britain*. Fontana. (Section 1 has some good articles on 'The Family')

4
Divorce

Some people suggest that a high divorce rate is a threat to the stability of the family. This chapter will examine the facts about divorce, look at the facts in the context of other social events, and finally try to interpret the facts, bearing in mind statements that have been made about the decline of the family.

The Divorce Rate

No one can dispute the fact that the divorce rate has risen dramatically during this century. The difficulty comes when we try to analyse the

Table 6
Number of Petitions filed for Dissolution and Nullity 1876–1976: England and Wales.

Remarks	Period	Number of Petitions (annual averages)
Period when working-class people were, in practice, denied access to the divorce court	1876–1880	460
	1881–1885	462
	1886–1890	556
	1891–1895	565
	1896–1900	675
	1901–1905	812
First World War	1906–1910	809
	1911–1915	1 033
	1916–1920	2 954
Poor Person Rules, 1925	1921–1925	2 848
	1926–1930	4 052
	1931–1935	4 784
Herbert Act, 1937	1936–1940	7 535
Hitler's War	1941–1945	16 075
Legal Aid, 1950	1946–1950	38 901
Divorce available	1951–1954	33 132
	1955–1960	27 617
	1961	31 900
	1966	46 600
Divorce Law Reform Act, 1969	1970	71 700
	1971	110 900
	1972	111 000
	1973	116 000
	1974	132 000
	1975	140 000
	1976	146 000

[Source: *Divorce in England* by O. R. McGregor (Heinemann); *The Registrar General's Statistical Review of England and Wales for the year 1967*, Part 2 (HMSO); *Social Trends* no. 4, 1973 and no. 9, 1979 (HMSO)]

causes of this increase or to come to some firm conclusion about the effect a high divorce rate has on the family as an institution.

This is a clear case of unexplained statistics being misleading without a certain amount of background information. In order to understand Table 6, it is necessary to have the following knowledge as well.

1 There has been an increase in population since 1876; so, looking at the *number* of divorce cases is less meaningful than knowing the percentage or the *rate* per 1000 marriages. In 1957, for example, McGregor estimated that only about 7% of marriages ended in divorce. Even if this was a slight under-estimate it was certainly a less dramatic or alarming way of looking at the problem. Since then, the percentage of marriages ending in divorce has increased, but it is still comparatively low.

2 Until 1857, divorce was a privilege of the rich, since it needed an Act of Parliament, costing about £800, to obtain a divorce. Even the 'cheaper' method after 1857 was out of the financial reach of the lower-middle and working classes. Cheap divorce was not really possible until the introduction of the 'Poor Person's rules' in 1920, and it became even more possible when a Legal Aid Scheme was introduced for the armed services during the 1939–45 war and for civilians after 1949.

3 Other important legal changes have made divorce a possibility for many more people. For example, until 1937 the only possible 'cause' for a divorce was adultery. The Matrimonial Causes Act of 1937 added three more causes: desertion, cruelty, and incurable insanity.

4 Since 1969 the idea of a matrimonial offence has been replaced by 'irretrievable breakdown' of the marriage as the only reason for divorce. This has once again widened the range of possible divorces.

To look at a set of divorce figures without weighing them against a changing legal, financial, and social scene can be very misleading. What then should be said about the relationship between divorce and family life? One point of view is that marriage ought to be indissoluble (i.e. completely permanent) and that the family ought to be stable. From this viewpoint divorce is certainly a threat. But we must be quite clear what we are arguing about: for anyone who believes that marriage is a contract made by God, and which should therefore never be broken under any circumstances, the figures I have quoted are completely irrelevant. But to say that marriage is a sacred contract and therefore 'unbreakable' is a theological point of view rather than a sociological one, and the question of evidence is then of no importance at all.

On the other hand, if a person believes that the family is being threatened by instability, then the evidence may be of value in testing the truth of the statement. In this case, however, we would have to balance the growing 'instability' in the family as the result of more divorces against the lower rate of instability as the result of less risk of one or more parents being removed from the family as the result of death. If we do this calculation, it appears that a family may be *more* stable in the twentieth century than in the nineteenth.

Another attack on divorce relies on the 'evidence' of what happens to the children of broken homes. This argument claims that divorce is not fair to the children. But what evidence is there about children of divorced families and the likelihood of delinquency or maladjustment? There is some evidence to support the view that the children of divorced parents are statistically more likely to become delinquents or need psychiatric treatment of some kind. I am talking here, of course, about *statistical probability*; that is, it is more likely that children from broken homes fall into this category of needing treatment of some kind; this does *not* mean that *all* children from broken homes become delinquent or neurotic, and it does not mean that all delinquent children come from broken homes! The correlation between divorced parents and children needing some kind of special attention is, however, high enough for us to look very carefully at the figures. It does appear to be the case that children stand a better chance of growing up normally in a harmonious family atmosphere, and there are plenty of case-studies available to confirm the common-sense suspicion that children (especially young children) may be 'damaged' by the uncertainty of a contested divorce or by the divided loyalties after a divorce has taken place. But once again, we have to look beyond the obvious or the 'common-sense': a very high proportion of divorces takes place where no children are involved, either because none have been born or because they are already grown up when the divorce is started. A second factor to be considered is that there is evidence in America which suggests that in families where husband and wife relations have virtually broken down but where no divorce takes place (perhaps because the parents stay together 'for the sake of the children'), the effect on the children may be just as bad or even worse than in the case of a divorced family. In such 'empty-shell' marriages, as they are sometimes called, the American research seems to show that the prolonged and unresolved tensions are even more difficult for children to cope with than clear-cut divorce. (This evidence is American, but we have no reason to believe that it might not apply to the situation in this country, though clearly we cannot be certain about this.)

The evidence, such as it is, does not seem to justify the conclusion that divorce should be made difficult or impossible, or even that divorce *causes* instability in the family: it is unsuccessful marriages which appear to be at fault. (Divorce may be the *result* rather than the *cause* of instability!) But neither does the evidence support the view that there is *no* connection between divorce and delinquency or maladjustment. Most people would be better pleased by a falling divorce rate than by a rising divorce rate. Can we take any measures to prevent more divorces? What do we know about the kind of marriages which are more likely to end in breakdown? Which couples are most likely to be divorce-prone? A significant factor, but one which couples have little control over, is – perhaps surprising – the religion of the husband and wife. Divorce is much less likely for Jews and Roman Catholics than for other denominations (but Roman Catholics make up for this by a rather high rate for desertion and separation). Mixed marriages also have a higher divorce rate than marriages within the same religious denomination. Social class differences are also significant:

Table 7
Divorces per 10,000 married women aged under 55 in each social class (1972),

Social class	
I	22
II	25
III N	43
III M	29
IV	25
V	51
All	30

[Source: 'The Association between Divorce and Social Class in England and Wales' by C. Gibson, in *British Journal of Sociology* 25, 79–93]

Another 'high-risk' category is those married young. Those who get married very young tend to be much more likely to be divorced. Teenage brides and bridegrooms are particularly prone to divorce. We should note that this is to some extent a purely statistical fact: a girl married at eighteen can expect to have a potential married life ten years longer than someone married at twenty-eight, or twenty years longer than a woman married at thirty-eight. This means that the eighteen-year-old is 'at risk' for divorce for a significantly longer period, and this alone would be enough to account for some difference in the divorce figures of the group as a whole. But this is not the complete story. Even taking the long-term risk into account, teenage marriages still seem to be less stable. This is *perhaps* because both partners might tend to be emotionally and socially less mature, and have the possibility of maturing away from each other (but this is speculation rather than evidence). It is also *possible* that for this age group (i.e. teenagers) a falsely romantic, unreal attitude to marriage is common, and that this may turn out to be an inadequate basis for marriage. Another possibly related factor is the high incidence of 'shot-gun' marriages among teenage brides, and in this case we can quote evidence rather than rely on speculation: in Great Britain about 30% of teenage brides are pregnant at marriage (compared with a figure of only 13% of brides aged twenty or more). It may be that necessity is not the ideal basis for marriage in all cases. Teenage brides are usually more likely to have to cope with difficulties about housing, perhaps sharing with in-laws, as well as general financial difficulties. One of the complicating factors here in interpreting the data is that more teenage brides and their young husbands are 'working-class' and would anyway tend to be less affluent and have to face a number of difficulties early on in their married life.

For whatever reasons, teenage marriages are about twice as likely to end in divorce as those of couples married in their twenties. In 1954, the Registrar General was confident enough to make this prediction: on the basis of current trends, he said that about one in four of women marrying at sixteen to eighteen would have been divorced by the twentieth anniversary of their marriage.

Apart from earlier marriages, there are a number of other reasons which might encourage the divorce rate to rise. One is the increasing emancipation of women – Victorian wives tended to do as they were told and not expect too much out of marriage; the more wives expect, the more they are likely to be disappointed, and the more likely it is that the marriage will become less harmonious. Another factor is the degree of mobility in our society, both social and geographical. There is a correlation between mobility and high divorce rates, so we might reasonably expect that the more mobility there is the more there is a tendency for divorce rates to rise correspondingly.

In surveying all of this evidence, we should maintain a sense of balance. There is no evidence that people today rush into marriage thinking that if it doesn't work out they can get a divorce. There is no evidence that a significantly higher proportion of marriages than fifty years ago fail today. Above all, there is no reason to believe that marriage is any less popular as an institution: more people get married today than ever before, and even those whose marriages break up through divorce tend to re-marry rather than 'retire from the field' in a disillusioned and embittered state. We have no reason to think that marriage and the family are on the way out.

Questions for Discussion and/or Written Work

I

a) Make a list of all the reasons that people put forward against making divorce easier.

b) Put a tick against those arguments which might be supported or refuted by evidence.

c) Summarise the relevant evidence that you know about and make a note of any evidence which you would like to have.

2 How would you explain the increase in divorce petitions in 1971? (N.B. A divorce petition is a *request* by a husband or wife to the court to grant a divorce: it usually takes a little time before the divorce becomes 'absolute'.)

3 What do you understand by an 'empty-shell' marriage? What do we know about children of such marriages? (N.B. Be careful not to imply *all* when you really mean *some*.)

4 Why do you think divorce is less common among Roman Catholics and Jews? Is your answer based on *speculation* or evidence? What is the difference between speculation and evidence?

5 What are the 'chances' of a teenage marriage ending up in divorce? (i.e. out of every 100 teenage couples married, about how many will still be married in twenty years' time?) Why are teenage marriages more likely to end in divorce?

6

'For this sample the working class revealed a higher number of teenage brides than the middle class, 33% as compared to 12%. 98% of the working class girls had married before they were twenty-five. 75% of the middle class had married before the age of twenty-five. Class differentials in marriage patterns have always existed, and at present probably reflect the different life patterns of young people. Middle-class adolescents who continue with their education are less likely to marry until they are at least twenty-one. It has also been suggested that the flight into marriage by the young working-class girl is perhaps her only way of acquiring the outward signs of adulthood and a limited and temporary limelight. ... Spinley (1953) has suggested that among the poorer working-class areas there is simply no place for an unattached woman, and the combination of this lack of status, with the general overselling of the delights of "falling in love" places enormous pressure on young girls to seek a mate.'

[Source: *The Captive Wife* by H. Gavron (Routledge & Kegan Paul)]

a) In Miss Gavron's sample, what percentage of working-class girls were still not married by the age of twenty-five? What percentage of middle-class girls?
b) What reasons can you suggest to explain the fact that working-class girls *tend* to get married younger than middle-class girls?
c) Do you think there is a great social pressure on girls in our society to 'fall in love' and 'find a mate'? Give some examples of the pressures.
d) Should it be regarded as 'normal' for girls to get married?
e) One woman in Miss Gavron's sample said 'I wouldn't advise others to marry so young', and 35% of the working-class wives in the sample felt they had married too young. If there are so many regrets afterwards, why is early marriage still so common? What are the advantages and disadvantages?

Further Reading

McGregor, O. R. *Divorce in England*. Heinemann
Central Statistical Office. *Social Trends*. HMSO
Sillitoe, A. F. *Britain in Figures*. Penguin

5
The Sociology of Education

In 1944 a very important change took place in our educational system – a change so important that it would be difficult to exaggerate its *potential* influence, although the effect of the 1944 Education Act has been disappointing in its concrete results in schools.

Why was the 1944 Act so important? Throughout the nineteenth century, education was divided rigidly along social-class lines: public schools for the upper and middle classes; elementary schools for the 'lower orders'; some grammar schools and independent schools for those in-between, or at least some of them. The various kinds of schools were quite different in their intentions, and in what was taught. Public schools kept their pupils, mainly boarders, until they were eighteen or nineteen, and their aim was to produce Christian gentlemen who would be the future leaders of society at home or in the Empire. In the first half of the nineteenth century, elementary schools were explicitly for the lower classes, who were expected to leave at the age of ten or eleven after receiving 'sound and cheap elementary instruction' in reading, writing, and arithmetic. As time went on, the school-leaving age was raised, so that by the 1930's it was up to fourteen, and the curriculum had widened to some extent; but the idea that only elementary or very limited education was suitable for the majority of the population continued, despite protests from the Labour Party and the TUC, especially during the 1920's and 1930's.

Whether a child went to a public school until he was eighteen or an inferior elementary school until he was fourteen had nothing to do with his ability or intelligence: it depended entirely on money or social class. Some areas were fortunate in the nineteenth century in that they had a local grammar school, probably a charitable foundation, which could take a small number of children and provide them with an education up to the age of sixteen or eighteen; but most of the children who benefited from these schools were middle-class, not working-class.

The educational opportunities for most working-class pupils were very limited.

At the end of the nineteenth century there was a shortage of men sufficiently well educated to fill all the clerical jobs which were necessary in England – which had become the industrial and commercial centre of the world. To meet the growing need for more grammar schools, the 1902 Education Act permitted local education authorities to build their own secondary grammar schools out of the rates, with some government assistance. (These were often called 'county' schools, as many of the local education authorities were counties.) The idea was that most of the pupils transferring to these schools at the age of eleven would be fee-payers (once again the children of middle-class parents), but it was also laid down that a proportion of places would be reserved as free places for extremely gifted children who would be selected on the basis of winning a scholarship. This remained the situation until 1944. The number of children who went to grammar schools was small (about 10%), the number of scholarship free places much smaller, and the number of working-class scholars very small indeed.

Throughout the 1920's and 1930's, two charges were repeatedly made about secondary education in this country. The first was that there should be *more places*; secondly, the charge was made that working-class children were not getting their *fair share* of scholarship places – even the grammar-school free places were often being taken up by middle-class pupils. To meet the second of these criticisms, some authorities introduced intelligence tests which were designed to select the bright working-class children rather than the less bright wealthier children who had been coached to pass an examination. But this only scratched at the surface of the problem – the real trouble was that the educational system at this time, far from levelling out inequalities, was sharpening them; that is, the education system was actually making it more difficult for working-class children to 'succeed'.

The Second World War (1939–45) provided an opportunity for some reformers to make plans for the post-war years in many important respects. The Beveridge plan for a Welfare State was one kind of forward-looking plan, the 1943 White Paper on Education and the subsequent Education Act of 1944 were other examples. But ideals do not always become reality simply by an Act of Parliament – especially when the Act is vague or ambiguous in some respects. So, many people who in 1944 were enthusiastic about the new Education Act later on became very disappointed when it seemed that many opportunities had been missed.

The major achievement of the 1944 Act was to legislate for free secondary education for all children; as part of this plan, the compulsory school-leaving age was to be raised from fourteen to fifteen, and then to sixteen as soon as practicable. As a result of the Act, elementary schools disappeared, and fee-paying in secondary schools was abolished. (Various kinds of 'independent' schools, of course, continued to exist and charge fees.) All children were to be sent to primary school from age five to eleven, and then to a secondary school from eleven to fifteen or up to eighteen. All children were, according to the Act, required to have an education suitable for their 'age, aptitude, and ability'. An education suitable for their age has never really presented any difficulty, but the interpretation of the phrase 'aptitude and ability' has caused endless arguments in education ever since.

According to the English educational system, it is for the central government to make general laws and regulations about education and for the local education authorities to carry them out. This is the idea of partnership between central and local government: a partnership which is both financial and a sharing of responsibility. It soon became clear, however, that the central government's legislation in 1944 was being interpreted very differently in various parts of the country. A few local education authorities set up comprehensive schools for all 'aptitudes and abilities', a few others set up comprehensive schools but retained some grammar schools and therefore a selection system to allocate bright pupils to them (such comprehensive schools are sometimes referred to as 'creamed comprehensive schools', and are therefore not truly comprehensive at all), but most local education authorities interpeted the 'aptitude and ability' wording to mean different kinds of schools for different kinds of ability. This was not surprising, since very similar recommendations had been made by two official government reports – the Spens Report of 1938 and the Norwood Report of 1943. So most local education authorities assumed there were three kinds of children, who could be sorted out by tests: academic pupils, who would go to secondary grammar schools; quite clever but rather more practical children, who would be selected for technical schools; and the rest, who would go to secondary-modern schools. This system became known as the 'tripartite' system of secondary education.

An essential part of the tripartite system (in theory) was that the three kinds of school were different but *equal* – the doctrine of 'parity of esteem' or 'parity of prestige'. According to this doctrine, no one should be regarded as inferior or as a failure if selected for a secondary-modern school – all children were still equal, but different.

This never really worked in practice. Why?

Criticisms of the Tripartite System

1 Despite parity of prestige, most parents (and especially middle-class parents) wanted their children to go to grammar schools. Grumbles about the results of selection tests at the age of eleven became very common. It also turned out to be much more difficult than had been expected to select the three types of child at eleven. Studies began to accumulate about extremely bright children who failed to pass into grammar schools, and also about many other children who were selected for grammar schools but became misfits. Then educationists and psychologists began to cast doubts on the use of tests in order to make final judgments about children at the early age of eleven. They suggested that tests were not accurate enough, and also that a person's IQ can change. Without an efficient testing and selecting system, the tripartite idea was not really workable.

2 The supposed advantage of partnership by which local education authorities were able to be different from each other turned out to be a serious disadvantage in this respect: it was soon discovered that whether a child got into a grammar school or not was not so much a matter of his intelligence as a question of geography. Over the country as a whole, about 20% of eleven-year-olds went to grammar schools, but in some areas there were places available for less than 10%, and in other areas over 40% of children could go to grammar schools. This made people question the fairness of the whole selection process.

3 Another kind of unfairness was also pointed out, especially by sociologists who made a number of surveys and other studies. Although the position had improved since fee-paying was abolished after the war, the 'chances' of a working-class boy or girl going to a grammar school was still much lower than the chances of middle-class children. Some research showed that this was because middle-class children did better in the tests; but this only prompted the obvious question, 'How fair are the tests?' (See Table 9 in Chapter 6.)

4 Finally, the whole idea of parity of prestige collapsed. As Olive Banks pointed out in her book *Parity and Prestige in English Secondary Education* (1955), it was not possible to keep up even a pretence of parity of prestige and say that secondary-modern schools were not regarded as inferior to grammar schools when quite clearly employers and adults in society generally valued the products of those schools (i.e. the pupils) differently. Olive Banks' argument was that, in a society which gives higher prestige to lawyers, doctors, and managers (the products of public schools and grammar schools) than to the carpenters, bricklayers, or dustmen produced by secondary-modern schools, the schools themselves which had produced these workers would also be

given high or low prestige according to the prestige of the 'products' of the school. Technical schools did not really catch on in most local education authorities, so for most children the choice was to try to get to a grammar school of high prestige or 'fail the 11+' and go to a low-prestige secondary-modern school.

The ideal of equality of opportunity was simply not compatible with the tripartite system (or in most cases, where there were no technical schools, the bipartite system).

The Growth of Comprehensive Schools

All these criticisms of the tripartite system encouraged more local authorities to move away from selection to the idea of comprehensive secondary schools. In recent years the debate about comprehensive secondary education has become openly political, so that the Labour Party is roughly committed to a policy of extending a good education to more people, whereas the Conservative Party emphasises the importance of providing an excellent education for the most able children, who will be the future industrialists, scientists, and professional workers without whom, they say, the country will not survive at all. It would be a mistake, however, to see this debate simply as a party-political matter; attitudes to priorities in education do cut across party lines to some extent.

The choice in education today is mainly this: do we want to put a high priority on providing a good education for everyone and try to give 'secondary education for all' a genuine meaning, or do we want to provide education for some and much-lower-level training for the majority? The first alternative is sometimes referred to as the '*egalitarian*' viewpoint, or wanting equality in education; the second alternative of concentrating our educational resources on the future top people in society is the '*elitist*' point of view. The kind of elitism referred to above would to some extent differ from the nineteenth-century educational elitism, which was providing for a social elite. The elite recommended for priority now might be an intellectual elite (i.e. the very intelligent) rather than a social elite; but, in practice, many of the advocates of an elitist system would expect the two elites to coincide to a very great extent, or they would hope to use the educational system to make sure that the social elite continued to have access to top positions.

Both of these kinds of policies have their built-in difficulties. The egalitarian view has as one of its aims a less socially divided or divisive country, where there are no great gulfs between one social group and another. Advocates of this ideal stress not just equality of opportunity, but a common educational experience for all children, and they would see an important purpose of education to be the transmission of a common culture. But what is this common culture? Can it be transmitted to everyone? These kinds of problems are quite difficult to solve in practice.

On the other hand, the elitist policy has great problems and difficulties too. How could the elitists prevent a division of society into the highly privileged and the under-privileged educationally? How can this policy be reconciled with the country being supposedly a democracy, with ideals of equality and social justice? If we want an intellectual elite, how do we select the members of the elite? Could it ever be really fair?

This last problem is very important in discussions about education in England, and leads us on to a consideration of what is meant by intelligence and ability. These terms are surrounded by all sorts of difficulties and problems.

The Nature of Intelligence

When psychologists and sociologists use the word 'intelligence', they use it in a more specific way than in general conversation, but even so they have found it necessary to distinguish between three different kinds of intelligence, which are sometimes referred to as Intelligence A, Intelligence B, and Intelligence C. Intelligence A is used to mean a maximum innate or inborn capacity, inherited *genetically* by a child from his parents: this determines his maximum learning power. Psychologists suggest that logically this maximum capacity must exist, although we can *never* measure it. They suggest that there must be for every individual a maximum intelligence that he could develop (given the right opportunities), just as every individual must be born with a maximum height potential (although he may not ever reach it).

Intelligence B is closer to our common-sense use of intelligence: a child is 'intelligent' if he is bright or clever, good at understanding, reasoning, or seeing relationships. Psychologists have sometimes referred to this as 'general mental efficiency'. This kind of intelligence is, of course, the result of a mixture of Intelligence A, which a child inherits genetically, and the child's social environment – i.e. his opportunities for developing his mental abilities.

Finally, Intelligence C is what we are able to measure by means of an intelligence test. If it is a good test, Intelligence C will give us a good idea of what a child's Intelligence B is, but not necessarily what his Intelligence A is. The reason for this apparent discrepancy is that Intelligence A is defined in terms of genetics – pure innate ability. Intelligence B is the result of that pure ability and the social environment, especially the family and the school itself.

In other words, we can never know what a child's real maximum capacity is, and it might be wise always to assume that a child could do better than his intelligence-test score indicates. This is a very great problem for those who want to select an intellectual elite: we can never be quite sure how much of a child's performance, even in an intelligence test, is due to his heredity or to his environment (and for this purpose his environment includes the kind of teaching he has received up to the point of the test). For this reason, no test can be completely fair.

Two more points need to be stressed about the nature of intelligence. The first is that Intelligence B (and this is what people normally mean when they use the word 'intelligence') is *not* fixed for life – if a child's environment changes (including his school, or even his stream or class) his IQ score *may* rise or fall. Secondly, Intelligence B does not show itself in the same way in all cultural groups: different kinds of environment will demand different kinds of 'intelligence'. One of the world's experts on intelligence, the British psychologist P. E. Vernon, has suggested that the group of skills which we call intelligence is a European and American middle-class invention. He suggests that sub-cultures such as the lower working class or rural groups develop different forms of intelligence. Also, people in very different cultures, such as the Australian aborigines or the Kalahari bushmen, display their intelligence in ways very different indeed from what we mean by intelligence in our society. People we regard as very clever in England would find that if they were stranded in the desert they would need other kinds of cleverness to survive.

Also, if we are talking about Intelligence C, that is, the score in a test of some kind, we should also remember that the test can be of no more than a *sample* of skills; therefore it may be a very incomplete picture of ability.

From the point of view of education and intelligence testing, we should always remember that, if someone achieves a low score in an intelligence test, this may mean that he is not very intelligent (in terms of Intelligence A or B); but it may also mean that he has not been exposed to the most favourable environment possible – including school environment; or it may mean that the test used did not give him adequate opportunity to reveal his Intelligence B. As we shall see, there have been a number of studies to show that most intelligence tests are not really 'fair' to some working-class children in this country, or to the negro population in various parts of the USA.

It would always be safer and fairer to assume that pupils are capable of improving their performance, rather than that they have reached their maximum performance. As a result of various studies, we do know something about 'good environments' as compared with 'bad environments' (when discussing this very limited question of intelligence – which may not be all-important anyway), but we do not know nearly enough. Social class, ethnic group, the size of family that a child comes from, as well as his position in that family, the school itself, and the personality of the teacher all appear to be factors of some importance. But we do not yet have a complete theory of what the best environment would be for producing intelligent behaviour or high educational performance. As regards the possibility of improving intelligence by deliberate educational programmes, there is some dispute over the evidence about the effectiveness of such programmes as the Headstart programmes in the USA. These have not been as successful as their supporters had originally hoped, but it is possible, and even probable, that some children have improved their IQ score significantly (together, presumably, with their capacity for benefiting from formal education).

But IQ improvement is not the most important factor. The real question is, given that people are of different levels of intelligence, how much does that affect their educability? In particular, how great a handicap is a below-average intelligence? The evidence which would be useful from Headstart programmes and other similar programmes in this country, such as the Educational Priority Areas Programmes, would be not how much children's IQ scores went up, but how much their educational performance was eventually improved by intensive learning programmes in the pre-school years. Unfortunately, this kind of long-term evaluation is much harder to organise, and even to measure, and therefore at the moment this kind of data is almost entirely lacking.

Questions for Discussion and/or Written Work

1 'It is not proposed that the children of the poor should be educated in a manner to elevate their minds above the rank they are destined to fill in society'. (Patrick Colquhoun, an educational reformer, 1806.)

This view was common in the early nineteenth century. Another reformer, Hannah More, wanted all children to be able to read so that they could be introduced to the bible; but she said that writing was unnecessary, and even undesirable, since it might upset the social order.

a) Why do you think the upper and middle classes were uneasy about providing education for working-class children in the early part of the nineteenth century?
b) Do you think some people still think in a similar way today?
c) Have you any evidence for your opinions?

2 After the 1944 Education Act, most local education authorities developed a 'tripartite' system of secondary education. The three parts of this system were secondary-grammar, secondary-technical, and secondary-modern schools.

a) Why was it then believed to be necessary to have three kinds of secondary school?
b) What were the differences between the three types of school?
c) What was meant by 'parity of prestige' or 'parity of esteem'?
d) Why did this policy of parity fail?
e) What replaced the tripartite system?

3 A comprehensive secondary school takes children of all abilities. They have been accepted in other countries, such as the USA and Sweden, but have been argued about a good deal in the UK.

a) Why?
b) What are the advantages and disadvantages of comprehensive schools?
c) Do comprehensive schools automatically produce greater equality? If not, what else is needed?

4
a) What do most people mean when they say that someone is 'intelligent'?
b) What are the *three* different meanings that psychologists and other social scientists give to the word 'intelligence' (sometimes referred to as Intelligence A, B, and C)?

5 Intelligence tests are sometimes used to arrive at a child's Intelligence Quotient (or IQ). If a child is exactly average he will have an IQ of 100, if he is below average in the test he will be given an IQ of less than 100, and if he above average his IQ will be more than 100.

IQ is worked out in a fairly simple way. If a child can solve problems which on average are typical of older children, he is said to have a *mental age* older than his actual age (or *chronological age*). So if a boy of ten could answer questions more like the average twelve-year-old, he would be said to have a mental age of twelve (and an IQ of 120). The exact MA (mental age) is worked out carefully by the test tesults, and the exact IQ is then worked out by the following formula:

$$\frac{\text{mental age (MA)}}{\text{chronological age (CA)}} \times 100 = \text{intelligence quotient}$$

Using the same example as before, MA = 12, CA = 10

$$\frac{12}{10} \times 100 = 120$$

a) What are some of the arguments against using IQ tests to select eleven-year-old pupils for grammar schools?
b) Why do some people say that intelligence tests are unfair to some kinds of children?
c) For what reasons were intelligence tests first used in English schools?
d) In New York, IQ tests were declared illegal. Why do you think this happened?

6 The following is an extract, reproduced by permission, from an article entitled 'Why Should Society Reward Intelligence?' by Jeffrey Gray, in *The Times*, 8 September 1972.

'The usual answer to this question is that we have to give superior ability extra rewards because otherwise those who possess it would not use their ability as society needs. But this theory does not stand up to careful scrutiny. It supposes that, in the absence of differential rewards for high IQ jobs, there would be fewer people with a high IQ offering to do those jobs. But how could this happen? It cannot be that high pay acts as an incentive for people to acquire a high enough IQ to do the job, precisely because IQ is largely determined at conception. Thus it could only be because people with a high IQ would really rather do a job requiring only a low IQ, and are persuaded otherwise by financial considerations. But there is no reason to suppose that this assertion is correct; indeed, it is not even plausible. How many engineers would choose to work on the assembly line, if only the pay was the same? At the least, the onus of proof rests with supporters of incentives.

Thus the evidence for genetic control of IQ cannot justify the fact that upper and lower classes are paid differently for the jobs they do. On the contrary, it suggests that this policy is a wasteful use of resources in the guise of "incentives" which either tempt people to do what is beyond their powers or reward them more for what they would do anyway. If we are ever to frame a rational incomes policy, this might not be a bad place to begin.'

a) Do you think the author believes that some people are more intelligent than others?
b) What is the usual argument for paying able or clever or intelligent people more than the average?
c) What does the author suggest is wrong with this argument?
d) What kinds of people would be most likely to oppose Gray's argument?

Further Reading

King, R. *Education*. Longman
Silver, H. (ed.) *Equal Opportunity in Education*. Methuen
Cowie, E. E. *Education*. Methuen
Hutchinson, M. E. *Education in Britain*. Hamish Hamilton

6
Social Differences in Education

Social Class and Educational Opportunity

I have already mentioned that during the 1930's one criticism of the educational system was that working-class boys and girls were deprived of educational opportunity – too few of them got to grammar schools. After the 1944 Education Act the situation certainly improved, but not enough to wipe out inequality in opportunity:

Table 8
Social origins of boys entering Secondary-grammar schools before and after 1944, England and Wales

Occupation of fathers	In percentage	
	1930–41	1946–51
Professional and managerial	40	26
Clerical and other non-manual	20	18
Manual	40	56

[Source: 'Social Class Factors in Educational Achievement' by J. Floud, in *Ability and Educational Opportunity* ed. A. H. Halsey (OECD)]

The above statistics do not look so much of an improvement if we remember that the boys of professional and managerial parents made up only about 4% of the total age group and yet got 26% of the grammar-school places even after 1944. Some people have suggested that this kind of inequality is inevitable because middle-class children are more intelligent and do better in the tests. Is this the real explanation? The Crowther Report in 1959 finally demolished this argument by showing that, even when ability *is held constant*, the chances of getting a selective secondary education rise or fall according to the social class of the pupil's parents. The Crowther evidence was based on a survey of eighteen-year-old National Service recruits in the late 1950's. The National Servicemen were tested on a battery of ability tests and then divided into six 'ability groups': Table 8 gives the results for the top two ability groups:

Table 9
Social-class Differences in the Schooling of Army Recruits (1956–58) at Two Levels of Ability

	Father's Occupation				
	Professional and managerial	Clerical and other non-manual	Skilled manual	Semi-skilled manual	Un-skilled manual
Ability Group 1					
	%	%	%	%	%
Independent or grammar schools	89·4	86·8	76·0	77·0	55·0
Technical schools	6·8	7·5	10·8	9·0	22·2
All selective schools	96·2	94·3	86·8	86·0	77·2
Ability Group 2					
Independent or grammar schools	58·6	32·4	22·1	18·0	14·0
Technical schools	10·5	14·2	11·0	11·3	12·3
All selective schools	69·1	46·6	53·1	29·3	26·3

[Source: Compiled from Table 2a, *15–18* ('The Crowther Report') Vol. II (HMSO)]

This Table shows that, even among the most able group (roughly the top 10%), working-class pupils were less likely to get to a selective school, even if we include those going to technical schools; but in Ability Group 2, social-class differences are even more marked.

The Crowther Report was particularly critical of an educational system which permitted so much *wastage of talent* or *uneducated capacity* – some of it from the top ability group but even more of it from the second ability group. It was found that social class was not the only factor, although it was very important. The education of the parents of the boys involved was also found to be important. (It seems to be the case that the more education parents have had, the more they want their children to have.) Size of family was also significant – children from large families were much less likely to go to grammar school or to stay on at school after fifteen.

The task of the Crowther Report was to make recommendations about the education of the fifteen to eighteen age group. Perhaps one of the most important conclusions was that *the education of the majority of*

Table 10
Contrasts in the Occupational Composition of the Grammar School-Leavers up to and over 16

School composition

Parental occupational group	Leavers up to 16	Leavers at 17 and 18
	%	%
Professional and managerial	17	39
Clerical and other non-manual	17	20
Skilled manual	51	34
Semi-skilled manual	9	5
Unskilled manual	6	2
	100	100

[Source: *15–18* ('The Crowther Report') Vol. II (HMSO)]

the population was inadequate both in its quality and in its duration: the majority of fifteen-to-eighteen-year-olds were not receiving any education at all. The social-class basis of the distribution of educational chances can also be seen from Table 10.

The same point was returned to in the Newsom Report of 1963, *Half Our Future*, which was concerned with average and below-average pupils. In their introduction to the report itself, the writers said, 'We are concerned that the young people whose education we have been considering should receive a greater share of the national resources devoted to education than they have in the past.' The Report also made a comparison between children of average and below-average ability in secondary-modern schools and those of similar ability who were being educated in independent schools. 'There is some evidence that young people with the same ability who attended recognised private schools and remained there in small classes until well beyond the statutory leaving age can achieve standards very different from those normally found.'

The conclusion that we have to come to is that we are still a long way away from getting the kind of equality of educational opportunity promised in 1944. In recent years the tendency has been for sociologists to turn away from the kind of 'demographic' surveys quoted above, which quote figures to show that working-class children are under-represented in grammar schools or even in the top streams of comprehensive schools; now the tendency is to ask questions about *why* working-class children appear so often to be the under-achievers. We have already seen that, apart from the inequality of getting places either in grammar schools or the top streams of comprehensive schools, there is the problem of whether the tests at 11+ and other ages are fair to working-class children. It seems extremely doubtful that they are fair. Most teachers and educationists and psychologists who set the tests tend to aim them at middle-class children – however hard they try not to! Other studies have shown that the language of working-class children, although perfectly adequate for communication in their own environment, is much less close to the language of education, especially to the language used in secondary education in textbooks, and even by the teachers themselves. It seems, therefore, that, consciously or unconsciously, middle-class teachers in schools are less helpful to children of working-class backgrounds than they need to be. It was partly for this reason that the Newsom Report recommended that all teachers should study sociology as part of their training for teaching in schools – they need to have an understanding of the culture and social background of their pupils. It is always tempting to see a cultural difference as a kind of inferiority: people generally tend to do

this when they see foreigners behaving differently, and teachers sometimes react in a similar way to working-class behaviour.

The problem of opportunity and equality in education has also
shifted in another direction. It is now suggested that, if we really
believe in equality in education, we must concentrate on providing
some kind of common curriculum in secondary schools. If children
in the top streams of comprehensive schools or in grammar schools
receive education which is different in kind (not simply in method of
teaching) from those in the lower ability groups, then this may mean
that some children are being denied access to important knowledge.
They may be prevented from getting the kind of knowledge which is
important not only for getting good jobs but also for a real understanding of the world in which we live. If, for example, some children study
physics and chemistry but others do a project on the local gasworks, we
have to ask whether both groups are eventually going to achieve a
genuine understanding of the scientific world in which we live. If
not, it looks as though some children are being 'sold short' in education.

The Purpose of Education

Such discussions as these inevitably lead us to questions about the
purpose of education. What is education really meant to do for us? An
important distinction might be that real education is much more than
just training people to acquire basic knowledge and skills which would
be necessary to get jobs. Genuine education means that a young person
should acquire a thorough knowledge and understanding of the adult
world. In our society, this would include a knowledge of mathematics,
science, and technology – as well as an understanding of the history of
our society and its political, economic, and social structure. Some of
the most important aspects of education in this sense might have very
little to do with getting a job at all. Getting a good job is very important
– but it is not the only important thing in life! Unfortunately many
young people seem to have been given a too limited view of the purpose
of education; this can be seen from Table 11, taken from a survey
called *Enquiry 1*, conducted by the Schools Council.

Formal and Informal Education

In many simple, pre-literate societies all education can take place within
the family or by informal contact with adults, often relatives; schools
are not needed. In complex industrial societies, for a number of reasons,
education has become formalised, that is, schools have been established
and professional teachers have been trained to make sure that certain

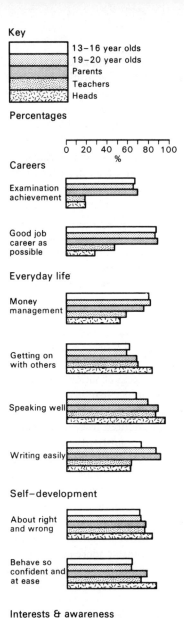

Key

- 13–16 year olds
- 19–20 year olds
- Parents
- Teachers
- Heads

Percentages

Careers

Examination achievement

Good job career as possible

Everyday life

Money management

Getting on with others

Speaking well

Writing easily

Self–development

About right and wrong

Behave so confident and at ease

Interests & awareness

Spare time interests, hobbies

Drama

Table 11
What school is for: attitudes of pupils, parents, and teachers

aspects of the society's culture get passed on to the next generation. Some sociologists have suggested that any kind of education anywhere has three aspects: first, the *technical*, that is, learning certain skills which are thought to be necessary for adult life and 'earning a living'; secondly, the *social* – trying to make sure that the individual will be able to play his part as a member of a larger community (i.e. a group bigger than his own family); and finally the development of character, that is, passing on certain *attitudes and values* which are particularly esteemed by that specific society. These may be religious values but are probably wider than that. Clearly, the part played by a formal institution like a school is a limited one. Even in an industrial society, a great deal of everyone's education must take place outside the school. For this reason, sociologists often make a distinction between *formal education* inside schools and colleges etc. and *informal education* which takes place in the family, in the peer group, and in the wider community – generally including a great deal of information and attitudes which reach individuals through the mass media.

It seems that in our society neither the family nor the school is sufficient to meet all the needs of young people. There seem to be two main reasons why the family cannot do everything that is needed educationally. The first reason is that in our kind of society parents are usually not very powerful as providers of occupational and social placement, partly due to the high rate of social mobility. In other words, fathers cannot always provide their children with all the knowledge and skills they need for their adult occupations. The second reason, connected to some extent with the first, is that society is changing so rapidly that parents (and adults generally) cannot provide other kinds of knowledge that young people need or want: that is, not only the technical knowledge and skills but also information about sex, for example, or drugs. The views of adults on such topics are often treated with hostility or suspicion by the young. A third reason is that the family, as we saw in Chapter 3, has tended to concentrate more and more on the individual, personal needs of the child in recent years, and less on the preparation for the impersonal relationships typical in work and in wider society outside the family generally.

It is precisely to meet these needs (and some others) that schools are provided. But schools have been comparatively unsuccessful in meeting many of these needs, either because they do not try to or because they fail to reach some young people (especially working-class boys). Many adolescents appear to need a link with or way into the more impersonal wider society; where this is not provided by the school in an adequate or satisfactory way, it is likely that adolescents will seek the companionship of people of their own age or slightly older – the adolescent peer group. Young people who are unsuccessful at school tend to become more dependent on the peer group than boys who are successful in achieving what schools want them to achieve.

Youth Culture

These are some of the reasons for the development of a youth culture, but there may be other important explanations as well. One is that 'adolescents' now constitute a very profitable market to be exploited by the manufacturers of clothing, records, and anything else that this age group can be persuaded to buy. Mark Abrams has defined adolescents as the young *unmarried* people of both sexes between fifteen and twenty-four. This is quite a wide age range, which makes up about 10% of the population. Perhaps the word 'adolescent' is not really appropriate for so wide an age range – many unmarried twenty-three-year-olds, I am sure, would object to being referred to as adolescents – but we have no other word which adequately describes the group of young people Mark Abrams wants to discuss and what other people have referred to as 'youth culture'. The word 'youth' itself is also unsatisfactory and equally vague in its age range. But if we think about the fifteen to twenty-four age group and discuss it in Abram's terms, we find that not only is this group a fairly large one but it is also fairly affluent. The earnings of members of this group have increased much more than the real wages of adults over the last twenty years, and also members of this group are much more likely to be spenders on 'entertainment' goods than are married people of their age or older groups who have commitments such as housing and the cost of children which tend to use up the bulk of their earnings.

In countries like ours there is a tendency for youth groups to develop, and this tendency is assisted to a considerable degree by commercial interests who wish to make money out of a profitable section of the community. But whether we are right in calling this a youth *culture* is open to debate. The tendency of young people of this age to have similar tastes and habits should not be exaggerated; also, the idea that there is a 'generation gap' should be examined very carefully. Admittedly there is a tendency for young people to seek a distinctive style in speech, clothing, and music, but that does not in itself constitute a generation gap. The term 'generation gap' is in many respects unsatisfactory: what is meant by generation? Is it thirty years? Or is there a generation gap between a seventeen-year-old and a twenty-seven-year-old? Or should its use be confined to the difficulty of communication between the young person and his own parents? Until we tidy up the use of the phrase it might be better to avoid it altogether in sociological discussion.

Surely many adults share the younger members of society's tastes in pop music and clothing etc., so the whole question of youth culture and generation gap is open to argument.

A similar view suggests that· the idea of teenage rebellion against adult standards has been greatly exaggerated. For example, in 1966 a Gallup poll showed that only 0·2% of teenagers could be classified 'delinquent'; very few young people are sexually promiscuous, or addicted to hard drugs. At least two studies have shown young people to be extremely conformist in their behaviour – perhaps disturbingly so. Thelma Veness in *School Leavers* (1962) came to the conclusion that young people were very much like their parents in their attitudes, values, and aspirations. Similarly, the Latey Report used the fact that young people were generally 'sensible' rather than irresponsible to support the view that the voting age should be reduced from twenty-one to eighteen.

One sociologist (Musgrove, in *Youth and the Social Order*, 1964) who examined the differences between adults and teenagers suggested that the problem was often that the young were being rejected by adults, not that the young were refusing to accept adult standards. Another view put forward was that when young people appeared not to accept adult values it might often be a question of 'delayed acceptance' rather than final total rejection. The suggestion was that young people knew that they would eventually 'come round to the adult point of view' but would enjoy a period of 'rebellion' first.

Another important point to bear in mind is that it is very doubtful whether we would be justified in generalising about *all* young people as if they were identical in their tastes, interests, and rejection of adult standards. J. B. Mays has suggested a classification of six kinds of distinct adolescent sub-groups:

1 the roughs, toughs and delinquents;
2 the street-corner boys;
3 the beats and hippies;
4 the youthful idealists and political activists such as CND etc.
5 the newly affluent proletarians (e.g. mods, rockers, and greasers);
6 middle-class public-school and university rebels.

No work has been done on the detailed social composition of each of these groups, but there are obvious social-class differences in membership.

Further discussion about social class and young people will be included in the next chapter.

Questions for Discussion and/or Written Work

I

'It is now clear that the main inequalities in British education today are due to three factors: differences in social class, in sex, and in geographical location.

If you happen to have had the luck to have been born a boy in Cardiganshire, your father being in the professional (or managerial) class, your chance of achieving full-time higher education would almost certainly be about 80% – that is, of every ten children in this class, eight would achieve a higher education. If, on the other hand, you were born as the daughter of a semi-skilled or unskilled worker living in West Ham, your chance of reaching full-time higher education would probably have been less than 0·5%. I say "probably", because the figures are not based on a survey of the actual situation in these two areas as far as class and sex differences in opportunity are concerned; the assumption I have made is the not unreasonable one that these differences are the same in these two areas as they are in the country as a whole.

These figures quantify the extent of differences in opportunity at their extremest points; they show that the Cardiganshire middle class boy has roughly 180 times as much chance of reaching full-time higher education than the West Ham working-class girl; and this when the country has, in a formal sense, committed itself to a policy of equality of opportunity.'

[Source: Extract from 'Inequalities in Education' by B. Simon, an address given at the 1965 CASE conference]

a) What do you think Brian Simon was mainly worried about when he wrote the article?

b) The article was written in 1965. Have any improvements taken place since then?

c) Out of a thousand middle-class boys in Cardiganshire, how many would be likely to go to university or college? Out of a thousand working-class girls in West Ham, how many would be likely to go to university or college.

d) Does this difference in educational chances really matter?

2

The Unequal Start

The 17 000 babies born in the week March 3–9, 1958, were studied in a National Birthday Trust survey to improve maternity services. Six years later the National Children's Bureau managed to mount a study on the home background, health, and physical and mental development of the children at seven. Nearly 92 per cent. of the families were traced and agreed to take part. Cash permitting, the surveys will take place every four years, giving invaluable help to future policy-making in health, education and welfare. The story so far is told in *From Birth to Seven.* Dr Ronald Davie, deputy director of the National Children's Bureau, and co-author of the book with Professor Neville Butler and Harvey Goldstein, tells us some of the findings when the children were seven years old.

In the National Child Development Study the term 'Social Class' is used simply as a shorthand term to describe the job a child's father does; the classifications used are the same as the Registrar General's for census purposes. Broadly, occupations in Social Class I demand higher professional qualifications; Social Class II includes teachers and many higher civil servants as well as managers in commerce and industry; Social Class III is by far the biggest single group in the population, and is usually divided into a non-manual section (foremen, clerical workers, shop workers) and a skilled manual section. Social Class IV consists mostly of semi-skilled manual workers and Social Class V of unskilled manual workers. Social Classes I, II and III (non-manual) are usually referred to as 'middle-class' and the manual occupation groups are referred to as 'working class'. These groupings are important in the study because in our society the father's job is generally quite closely related to the kind of education he has had and to the whole life-style of the family. This is, of course, a considerable over-simplification but sharp differences do emerge between the classes. Every effort has been made to see that the study's findings take account of these differences and other important factors which might otherwise distort the results or produce misleading conclusions. For example, children in independent schools have very high educational attainments. But is this because of their schooling? Or their home background?

Are some children more equal than others?

The chances of an unskilled manual worker's child (Social Class V) being a poor reader at seven years old are six times greater than those of a professional worker's child (Social Class I). The chances of a Social Class V child being a non-reader at this age are 15 times greater than those of a Social Class I child. One explanation for this is the home background of most middle-class children; they arrive at school tuned in not only to the educational demands but also to the way they are expected to behave in school. The initial difficulties of some working-class children in acclimatising themselves sometimes result in alienation. Our results show that more working-class children, even by seven years of age, are showing hostility towards teachers or, worse still, withdrawal, depression and a 'writing-off' of adult standards. Also, although children are tending to get taller each decade, the gap between the classes is not narrowing. On average, children from Social Class I were found to be 1·3 in. taller than children from Class V. A similar national study 12 years ago showed practically the same difference. Families liable to need the medical and welfare services most were, we found, least likely to use them. In Social Class I, one per cent. of children did not go to a dental clinic or private dentist as against 31 per cent. in Class V. Scotland has a particularly poor record – as many as 13 per cent. of Scottish children had at least half their teeth decayed, missing or filled, compared with only 6 per cent. in the north Midlands, for example.

(Scotland is said to have the highest sweet consumption in the British Isles.) Speech difficulties are six times as frequent in Social Class V as in Class I; yet attendance for speech therapy is no higher in Class V. You might say that, as these services are provided, it is up to the parents to use them, but this would ignore the needs of the children. What we urgently want is more information on why some families don't use the clinics, and then see to it that the children do get their fair share.

What effect does housing have on reading?

We compared the attainments and adjustment of children whose family had the sole use of hot water, indoor lavatory and bathroom with those who didn't have them or shared them. Taking account of other relevant factors – such as class, family size and type of accommodation – the 'haves' were on average nine months ahead in reading. The 'have-nots' were also behind in arithmetic and were less well adjusted in school. Obviously you can't put in a bath and expect an immediate improvement in a child's reading. Yet bad housing conditions can lead to poor health, depression and irritability in parents and children; they may also produce a feeling of alienation from the more privileged sector of society (with which the school may be identified).

A similarly gloomy picture emerges from a comparison between the results of children living in over-crowded houses and those who didn't. The definition of overcrowding in our study was the same as that used by the Registrar General for the 1961 census. The total number of persons in the household is divided by the number of living rooms and bedrooms in the house; this ratio is used as an index of overcrowding. A kitchen is counted as a room only if it is used for eating (or sleeping). (In the 1966 census *all* kitchens were counted as rooms, thus lowering the overcrowding figure 'at a stroke'.) By the 1961 census definition, any child living in a household with more than 1·5 persons per room is considered to be overcrowded. This is in no way a luxury standard. The Milner Holland report, *Housing in Greater London*, 1965, thought it lagged far behind what was regarded as acceptable even by average sections of the community. For example, a family of husband and wife and four children having two bedrooms and two living rooms would *not* be overcrowded by this standard. We found the actual amount of overcrowding among seven-year-olds to be very high, 15 per cent. In Scotland nearly four out of every 10 of the children lived in overcrowded conditions.

Can you buy a good education?

Seven-year-olds in private schools do have much higher attainments than those in State schools. However, most of this academic superiority can be explained in terms of social class, and by differences in the standard of education of the children's fathers. Allowing for these two factors, the gap between private and State school closes: the better results of private schools are reduced to about four months in reading and six months in arithmetic. Our best guess is that, taking everything else into account, the remaining difference in reading and arithmetic would be marginal with perhaps a slight advantage to the private schools. It is doubtful whether any such advantage in school attainments could justify the additional costs. We shall be interested to see whether the follow-up on the children at 11 shows the same picture.

When is a habit bad?

When your parents disapprove. This answer is not so facile as it may sound because some habits are frowned upon in certain social groups and less so in others. About 8 per cent. of the children in Social Class I were reported at seven to be frequent nail-biters compared with 13 per cent. in Class V. On the other hand, there were only 5 per cent. frequent thumb-suckers in the working-class groups, but 10 per cent. in Social Class I. Does the relative popularity of dummies among working-class families explain the lower proportion of thumb-suckers? If so, perhaps parents who find the sight of a baby sucking a dummy displeasing should weigh this against any objections to later thumb-sucking! The arguments against the use of a dummy on hygienic, as distinct from dental, grounds have always seemed rather slender in view of the many other objects which inevitably find their way into young mouths.

One in nine children were reported to have been wetting their beds (more than the occasional mishap) after the age of five, boys being rather more likely to be bed-wetters than girls. Although this is by no means uncommon among young school-children, parents should take the opportunity of mentioning it to their doctor at a convenient time in case there is a physical cause which needs treatment. Soiling by day after four years of age was much less common (slightly over one in a hundred); this was reported to be three times as common in boys as in girls. For both bed-wetting and soiling there was an upward trend from Social Class I, reaching the highest proportions in Social Class V. Most parents would find the number of behaviour difficulties and bad habits reported to us reassuringly high.

Are allergies class-conscious?

Asthma, eczema and hayfever appear to have a lot in common. The causes are not yet completely understood but they are often reactions to allergic stimuli and sometimes to stress; it is not unusual for two or all three of the conditions to occur together in the same person, or occur in the family of an affected person. The mothers reported that 3 per cent. of the children had at some time had one or more attacks of asthma; 6 per cent. had had hayfever or sneezing attacks; and 5 per cent. had suffered from eczema even after the first year. The associations were very striking; of the children reported to have had one or more attacks of asthma, 30 per cent. had had eczema after the first year, 14 per cent. still had eczema on examination at seven years, whilst 35 per cent had had hayfever or sneezing attacks. More boys (4 per cent.) than girls (2 per cent.) were reported to have had one or more attacks of asthma; and there was also a sex difference for hayfever (boys 6 per cent.; girls 5 per cent.). There was no sex difference for exzema. Each of the allergic conditions was reported to be more prevalent in middle-class children than those from work-ing-class families, being approximately twice as high in Social Class I as in Class V. There was less in Scotland and the north of England than in Wales or in the south of England. The highest reported rates for asthma were in Wales (5 per cent.) and in southern England (4 per cent.); the lowest were in northern England (3 per cent.) and in Scotland (2 per cent.). A further analysis carried out in the case of asthmatic children showed that neither the national differences nor the area differences in England could be accounted for by class differences. Clearly the reasons for the social class gradient and the north/south variation in these disorders merit further investigation.

Which children are backward?

We were very encouraged to find that a single obstetric event like bleeding or toxaemia in pregnancy is rarely linked to a subsequent disability or handicap; but the presence of a small number of birth factors together (including several previous pregnancies, a shortened or prolonged pregnancy, low birthweight, unsupported mother and unskilled working-class family) can help to establish which children are at higher risk of developing a handicap later. There was least educational backwardness (2·4 per cent. overall) among children born at the 'normal' time, more among late births and twice as much among early births. Irrespective of the length of pregnancy, educa-tional backwardness was 11 times more common in the fifth or sub-sequent children of working-class families (13 per cent.) than in the first-born middle-class children (1·2 per cent.).

The proportion of handicapped children, or those thought by their teachers to be in need of special schooling, was increased among those mothers not attended by a trained person in labour. Knowing the warning signals in pregnancy and later can help both to pick out those children whose development should be monitored, and to prevent these adverse circumstances from occurring. Early detection of handicaps is vital so that they can be treated medically with the minimum of delay or, if this is not possible, the parents and child can be helped to cope with or compensate for the problem. As a matter of course, children should be taken regularly to a child health centre or well-baby clinic, usually held either by local authorites or a G.P. If the parents feel there is something wrong they should get medical advice right away.

[Source: *From Birth to Seven* by R. Davie, N. Butler, and H. Gold-stein (Longman); reproduced in *The Sunday Times Magazine*, 4 June 1972]

a) The authors suggest that one reason for greater numbers of working-class children being non-readers or poor readers is that middle-class children arrive at school 'tuned in' to what is expected of them at school.

What does this mean? Give some examples.

75

Why should there be a class difference of this kind? Are teachers to blame?

b) What are some of the other indications that working-class children feel less 'at home' in school?

c) Make a list of the other ways mentioned in the article in which middle-class children appear to be at an advantage.

d) What could be done to get rid of some kinds of 'unfairness'.

3

'For the majority of the children . . . the entry to grammar school was uncertain and confused. They had suddenly lost in some measure that mesh of securities, expectations, recognitions, that we have called "neighbourhood". "I had this feeling of not belonging anywhere," said Patricia Joy. They found themselves surrounded by more middle-class children than they had ever met before. These children spoke better, seemed more confident, some already knew bits of French and Latin, their father had told them what "Physics" was about, a few even knew the teachers. *They*, evidently, seemed to belong. This insecurity was heightened by confusions over getting the right books, the right sports equipment, the right uniform. "I didn't like it," said Rita Watson, "my uniform seemed too big all round – long sleeves – I suppose my mother had to do it like that so it would last longer, but I felt awful. All the other girls' uniforms seemed all right. *I* was wrong." On top of this came the new subjects, the new vocabulary (not "kept in" but "detention", not "playtime" but "break" – and was it "yard" or "playground" or "cloisters"?) the masters' gowns, the prefects, the whole body of customs, small rights and wrongs, that any well-developed grammar school holds. Some of the schools made a practice of teaching the new children aggressively for the first weeks, to "break them in", and, presumably, to nip behaviour problems in the bud. The effect on children already bewildered was to knock them off balance rather than "break them in" and to create, rather than cure behaviour problems . . . For some of the working-class children confused by a genuine loss of part of their social life ("neighbourhood"), perplexed by the strangeness and sheer difference of grammar school, conscious of new *social* barriers thickening the normal barriers between pupil and teacher, and unable to turn to parents for explanation and understanding – for these children the beginnings could seem almost hallucinatory "I had the feeling like when you were in the forces," said one boy, "after you got your jabs and you got inoculation fever, you felt away from it all. You felt in a bit of a haze, everything was a bit bleared. Well that's how school felt at first. I felt just as I did later when I'd got inoculation fever."'

[Source: *Education and the Working Class* by B. Jackson and D. Marsden (Routledge and Kegan Paul)]

a) Why was starting at the grammar school uncertain and confused?

b) What advantages did the middle-class children tend to have compared with working-class pupils?
c) Why was there a barrier between pupils and teachers?
d) What does this extract tell us about educational opportunity?
e) This extract is from a book about one particular school in the North of England and a sample of its ex-pupils. How valuable is this as evidence?

4 *'Education in Tribal Societies*

Though children are not brought up exactly the same way in all tribal societies, the general pattern of education is roughly the same in all simple communities. First, the children get the social, technical, and religious knowledge that equips them for later life. This training is quite general, and teaching is informal. In many such societies, the boys – and sometimes the girls – are prepared for initiation ceremonies, and they must then be specifically taught to submit to social discipline and to develop a deep reverence for their tribe's customs and beliefs. Thus, the education of each new generation is designed to preserve the group's traditions. To get a clearer picture of just how children in a tribal society are prepared for adulthood let us take a close look at the education system of the Zulus of South Africa:

Zulu mothers have to teach their daughters what they need to know. They show the girls how to till the fields, how to make cooking pots, and how to prepare and serve foods. The girls make themselves useful by fetching water and firewood. Boys are handed over to the care of men at the age of about six. They are expected to look after sheep and goats until they reach their teens, when they graduate to cattle-herding. A boy may also learn the craft practiced by his father or uncle, through watching and imitating the way, for example, he carves wood or shapes metal.

The children pick up social manners incidentally, but they are given very careful instruction about their rights and duties as members of their clan. The methods of teaching are simple: adults show and tell, strengthening the lessons with a smile or a scolding, a slap or a bit of food. All this primary education is quite informal, but it is taken very seriously by the parents, who spend a great deal of time with their children.

The second stage in the education of a Zulu boy or girl is closely related to the ceremonies that mark each step forward to adulthood. Each such ceremony has a prescribed ritual that helps to link the young person with the gods. Boys and girls are prepared in separate groups for the big turning points in their lives. Their parents hire coaches who live with the children in isolation huts for three months or more, strictly supervising their training. The youngsters get moral lessons in the form of fables and parables, and are taught the folklore and proverbs that all Zulus must know. Sacred rites are performed through which adolescent boys and girls learn the correct way to appeal and give thanks to ancestral spirits. Adults who are skilled in the use of traditional tools make incisions – often very painful – in the skin that leave decorative and symbolic scars. The children's teachers also make certain that the novices keep various taboos demanded for the initiation ceremony, such as avoiding certain kinds of food. The outcome of this stern training is that young people learn gradually how to feel and behave as adult Zulus should. They master their social roles through an education that is deeply religious and traditional.

In most tribal societies, education ends with these initiation ceremonies. But the Zulus have a more complex society than, for example, the Indian tribes of the Amazon valley. Zulus live in larger communities, their lineage groups have close relations with one another, and there is a sense of kinship extending to what might almost be called a Zulu nation. Because of this higher level of complexity, there is a third, higher level of education. The aim is to prepare selected men to take part in public and political affairs, by giving them a working knowledge of tribal laws and customs. The sons of noblemen and those of some commoners are invited to the court of the paramount chief, where they are given lodging and food at his expense. While these students receive no formal lectures, they do attend important law cases; through listening to the comments of counsellors and spectators, they learn how to form their own judgments.

Modern Zulus are no longer taught military skills. But in the days of the great chief Shaka (1783–1828), a still-revered leader and conqueror, these skills were considered extremely important. Young men, selected for their courage and physique, were sent to camps where experienced officers trained them in the skills of the warrior. They were taught how to use arms; how to move troops in attack or retreat; how to make use of the particular lay of the land; how to deal with the problem of food and arms supplies. The young soldiers were continually exposed to arduous and dangerous tests, designed to keep them physically fit and to develop their spirit of bravery. But military science and technique were also fused with religion: in the eyes of their teachers it was equally important that the young trainees should know what amulets to wear, what magic formulas to recite, and what foods to eat or avoid before battle.

Today, not only traditional Zulu education but tribal education everywhere is being replaced by formal schooling introduced by the dominant industrial nations – generally European. The resultant clash of cultures gets a mixed reception from tribal peoples.'

[Source: *Man in Society*, ed. M. Douglas (Macdonald)]

a) Read the passage about Zulu education and divide what a Zulu boy has to learn into the three categories mentioned in Chapter 6: (i) technical training, (ii) social education, and (iii) character development.
b) Today many Zulu children go to schools which have been provided for them, but why were schools unnecessary in traditional tribal life?
c) In what ways has your education been different from that of a Zulu?

5
'The grammar school ensures for most of those who pass successfully through it a relatively high social status in contemporary Britain.
It exacts a formidable price for this service. Although it carries high
prestige and has the confidence of the majority of parents at all
social levels, it systematically humiliates its pupils, reduces their self-
esteem, promotes uncertainties, ambiguities and conflicts in social
relationships, a negative – even a despairing – outlook on life and
society.
  This is the classic prescription for the production of an experimental and deviant minority. Experiment and deviation have not in
fact been remarkable among ex-grammar school pupils, particularly
since the end of World War II, partly because the social and economic
rewards which soon follow their chastening experiences have been,
if not spectacular, at least adequate. Young professional men and
women have never been so comfortable so early. But for many it
would seem that the very capacity for vigorous deviation, or response
of any sort, has been effectively paralysed by their schools. Drilled
in receiving opinions, carefully memorizing the steps which demonstrate established truths, the grammar-school boy only too often, as
Hoggart suggests, loses "spontaneity so as to acquire examination-
passing reliability. He can snap his fingers at no-one and nothing;
he seems to make an adequate, reliable, and unjoyous kind of clerk".'

  [Source: *Youth and the Social Order* by F. Musgrove (Routledge
  & Kegan Paul)]

a) What 'price' does the author suggest grammar-school pupils pay
   for high status? Is this just his opinion?
b) Why according to the author, do grammar-school pupils lack
   'deviation' and 'spontaneity'? Are these qualities important?
c) Does this passage fit in with your own experience?
d) This sounds more like a description of socialisation or training for
   obedience and conformity than real education. What is the difference?

6 *Intelligence Tests*
  'Intelligence tests have been constructed of three kinds. Verbal,
paper-and-pencil tests, non-verbal paper-and-pencil tests, where the
tasks are presented by means of pictures and diagrams, and performance tests which require the manipulation of objects. Some, such
as the Binet test and the performance tests, are given to subjects
separately; most verbal and non-verbal tests can be done by a group
of subjects writing at the same time.
  The subjects are told to do their tasks within a certain time, their
results are marked, and the results of each is compared with a scale
indicating what may be expected of children of the same age, i.e.
what marks are expected of the relatively few bright ones, what
marks are expected of the few dull ones, and what marks are
expected of the bulk of the population with whom the comparison

is being made. This "calibration" of the test has been made beforehand and we are not concerned with the methods employed. One thing, however, we have to notice, and that is the assessment of the intelligence of any subject is essentially a comparative affair.

The results of assessment are expressed in various ways, the most familiar being in terms of what is called the Intelligence Quotient. For our purposes we need not consider how this has been devised, it is enough to say that an IQ round about 100 is "average", while more than 105 or less than 95 are above or below the average respectively.

Now since the assessment of intelligence is a comparative matter we must be sure that the scale with which we are comparing our subjects provides a "valid" or "fair" comparison. It is here that some of the difficulties, which interest us, begin. Any test performed involves at least three factors: the intention to do one's best, the knowledge required for understanding what you have to do, and the intellectual ability to do it. The first two must be held equal for all who are being compared, if any comparison in terms of intelligence is to be made. In school populations in our culture these assumptions can be made with fair plausibility, and the value of intelligence testing has been proved up to the hilt. Its value lies, of course, in its providing a satisfactory basis for prediction. No-one is in the least interested in the marks little Basil gets on his test, what we are interested in is whether we can infer from his mark on the test that Basil will do better or worse than other children of his age at other tasks which we think require "general intelligence". On the whole such inference can be made with a certain degree of confidence, but only if Basil can be assumed to have had the same attitude towards the test as the others with whom he is being compared, and only if he was not penalized by lack of relevant information which they possessed.

It is precisely here that the trouble begins when we use our tests for people from different cultures. If, as happens among the Dakota Indians, it is indelicate to ask a question if you think there is someone present who does not know the answer already, this means that a Dakota child's test result is not comparable with the results of children brought up in a less sensitive environment. Porteous found difficulty among the Australian aborigines. They were brought up to believe that all problems had to be discussed in the group, and they thought it very eccentric to be expected to solve one by oneself.

Supposing, however, a satisfactory attitude towards the test can be assumed, what about equality in relevant knowledge? In a society where children play with bricks, performance tests involving the manipulation of little cubes present an easier problem than they would in a society where such toys were unknown. Bartlett reports that a group of East African natives were unable to arrange coloured pegs in an alternating series, but they planted trees according to the same plan in everyday life.

Then there is the story of the little boy in Kentucky who was asked a test question: "If you went to a store and bought six cents worth of candy and gave the clerk ten cents what change would you receive?" The boy replied: "I never had ten cents and if I had I wouldn't spend it on candy and anyway candy is what mother makes." The tester reformulated the question: "If you had taken ten cows to pasture for your father and six of them strayed away, how many would you have left to drive home?" The boy replied: "We don't have ten cows, but if we did and I lost six I wouldn't dare go home." Undeterred the tester pressed his question: "If there were ten children in your school and six of them were sick with the measles how many would there be in school?" The answer came: "None, because the rest would be afraid of catching it too."

Thus all intercultural comparisons of intelligence are vitiated by the lack of true comparability, and any generalization about "racial" differences in intellectual competence which do not take account of this are worthless. So are many comparisons which have been made between children of different social classes.'

[Source: *Social Psychology* by W. J. H. Sprott (Methuen)]

a) 'the assessment of intelligence is a comparative matter . . .' What does this mean?
b) How useful do you think intelligence tests are in schools?
c) Why was it difficult to test the intelligence of Dakota Indians in America? Can you think of any other difficulties?
d) Why does the author say that comparisons of intelligence between different social classes are 'worthless'?

Further Reading

Young, M. *The Rise of the Meritocracy, 1870–2033.* Penguin
Douglas, M. (ed.) *Man in Society.* Macdonald. (Chapter 12, 'Education')
Bourne, R. and MacArthur, B. *The Struggle for Education.* Schoolmaster Publication Co.

7
Social Roles
and Social Class

All societies have a system of social differentiation. In societies which are very close to subsistence level – that is, where people have to spend most of their time concentrating on survival – the socially different roles will tend to be few, and they will be very clear-cut. Age and sex are usually important as the basis of roles, and in a very simple social system they may be the only two factors. There are always certain jobs laid down as men's functions rather than women's, and there are always differences recognised between the young, and mature, and the old. These need not involve serious inequalities, but there is a widespread tendency in human societies for some individuals to be richer, more powerful, and of higher prestige than others. The role of child tends to be of low power and prestige, the role of wife tends to carry less power than a masculine role, and it is common in simple societies for leaders to have considerable power and prestige (even if they do not have greater wealth).

In industrial societies, where there is a more complicated economic system based on division of labour, the number of roles in society is vastly increased, and many of the roles – especially occupational roles – tend to be arranged in a ranking system and to be closely connected with wealth.

Every role carries with it a pattern of expectations as well as duties, responsibilities, and privileges. We expect a doctor to behave in a certain way; he, in turn, expects the patient to play the role of patient. This makes the interaction between the two easier in that particular social context; life would be intolerable if no one ever knew 'how to behave' in any social situation. On the other hand, if people *always* behaved exactly as expected, life would be boring and uninteresting: many novels and plays, as well as jokes and humourous situations, are based on people who consciously or unconsciously behave in a way which is reckoned to be inappropriate to the role they should be playing; for example, the caretaker in a school who behaves more like a headmaster, or Groucho Marx in *A Night in Casablanca*, who, as the new manager of a hotel, suggested that, once guests were booked in, all the numbers of the hotel rooms should be altered. 'Think of the confusion', said the assistant manager. 'Yes, but think of the fun' replied Groucho.

Stratification

Throughout most of history, inequality seems to have been accepted as part of the natural order. When some individuals began to think about it (for example medieval philosophers or Hindu Brahmins), they usually managed to justify the inequality in their particular society on religious grounds. In India the inequality of the caste system was justified by 'the law of Karma', which was the fatalistic doctrine of 'as a man sows, so shall he reap': the inequality in this life was justified in terms of behaviour in a previous incarnation. In a rather different way the medieval and later Christian writers thought that inequality was ordained by God, and that individuals would be judged according to their execution of duties in accordance with their positions in the hierarchy:

The rich man in his castle,
The poor man at his gate,
God made them high and lowly
And ordered their estate.
                    (Nineteenth-century hymn)

It is only in very recent times – especially since the Industrial Revolution and the American and French Revolutions – that social inequality has been analysed in a scientific and critical way.

I want now to consider social stratification as one kind of social differentiation, and then go on to look particularly at that method of social stratification – social class – which is prevalent in modern industrial societies.

The term 'stratification' is used when there exists in a society a *hierarchy* – i.e. a system of ranking individuals into groups which become layers or 'strata' in the system. The essence of stratification is that an individual's prestige and power depends on his position in the hierarchy – that is, the stratum or layer he happens to belong to. If that sounds very complicated, it may be clarified by a few examples. Sociologists have classified societies by three major types of stratification:

1 caste,
2 estate (e.g. feudal system),
3 social class,

(and some would add a fourth social system based on slavery).

As with many sociological classifications, it is important to remember that these are suggested as 'ideal types'; that is, they may not exist anywhere in a completely 'pure' form, but we can find examples of societies which are mainly one or other of these three or four categories.

1 Caste

Caste is the most rigid form of stratification and possesses the following characteristics:

a) The social groups are completely closed, so that there is no mobility possible from one group to another;
b) individuals are born into a position in the hierarchy – in sociological terminology this means that positions or statuses are all 'ascribed', rather than achieved;
c) the hierarchy is fixed and clearly defined (sometimes legally, sometimes by religious sanctions);
d) inter-caste marriage is normally prohibited.

The society which was nearest to this 'ideal type' of a caste system was pre-industrial India, but it is also true that some sociologists have referred to South Africa as a caste system (white, coloured, and Bantu or negro populations). And other sociologists have pointed out that in the deep south of the United States the social structure had many similarities to a caste system some years ago, when there were legal as well as social sanctions against inter-marriage; and it is of course impossible to change one's colour.

2 The Estates System of Stratification

In Western European feudal societies, stratification was based mainly on *land tenure*, and land was held by a subordinate in the social system who owed certain specific duties to his feudal superiors. These duties were mainly military, but there were also financial obligations; for example, in the English feudal system there were certain feudal aids due when the King's eldest son was knighted and when his eldest son or daughter was married. There were similar obligations lower down the hierarchy. The characteristics of a system of stratification based on estate would have been:

a) the hierarchy was clearly defined by law as well as by custom;
b) membership of any stratum would have been determined very largely by birth, but some limited mobility was always possible;

for example, promotion might be achieved by war service;
c) each stratum was comparatively closed, with little inter-marriage.

This system, the feudal system, never existed in a pure form in England, and was complicated by the existence of a parallel hierarchy in the Church; the bishops and abbots were also organised in strata, but mobility was possible in the hierarchy of the Church (a priest could become a bishop, and later an archbishop). The position in England was also complicated by the existence, from the twelfth century onwards, of rich merchants in towns, who were technically low in terms of stratification but were rich and powerful within their own towns. Some historians suggest that it was probably the growth of towns that was the most important force in changing the feudal system in England into a social-class system.

3 Social Class

The characteristics of the social-class system contrasted with the caste and estate systems are:

a) The basis of social class is primarily economic – that is, it is a question of wealth and income: how much money and where it comes from.
b) The separate strata are not clearly marked off from each other: the boundaries between social classes are vague.
c) Social class is not formally legalised: in theory, all members of society are equal before the law. In a feudal system this was not so – certain people were *legally* privileged.
d) Inter-marriage is possible in a social-class system. Compared with a feudal system, inter-marriage is much more common, but statistically relatively uncommon. Even where inter-marriage takes place it is not without its difficulties; for example, the chances of divorce are somewhat greater in this kind of inter-class marriage.
e) Mobility is an essential characteristic of the social-class system. People who say that we now live in a classless society because it is possible to move 'from rags to riches' misunderstand the whole basis of social class – they are probably thinking of a more rigid system such as the feudal system. It would be correct to say that we are no longer a feudal society, but it would be wrong to say that England is classless.
f) As a result of social mobility and a lack of clearly defined social-class boundaries, the various symbols of class are of importance. (For example, in the time of King Edward III the sumptuary laws

defined what clothes various ranks could and could not wear. Today there are no such *legal* prohibitions, but other symbols have become more important: 'correct' behaviour, 'appropriate' speech, etc.)

From the above description it is clear that in England we have a much less pure type of social-class system than in many other modern industrial societies: our system of stratification is basically one of social class, but we retain certain aspects of the feudal system such as legal titles like dukes and lords, certain privileges which the aristocracy retain, etc. This tends to confuse the issue when people discuss social class: they tend to think that, because the distinctions and the privileges of the aristocracy have become less important, the social-class system is losing significance. In fact the opposite is the case – as the feudal system declined, so a system of stratification based on social class gradually took over.

Karl Marx

A great deal of recent sociological discussion about social class has been centred around the ideas of Karl Marx. Marx's view of social class was that it was basically an economic phenomenon; for Marx, an individual's social class had to be defined in terms of his relationship to the means of production, in other words, his ownership or non-ownership of that kind of property which is a source of income that can be used for creating more wealth.

Marx, writing about England in the nineteenth century, spoke of three groups: *land-owners, bourgeois* entrepreneurs (capitalists), and the *proletariat* (the peasants and workers). An essential feature of class was that the landowners and the bourgeois capitalists possessed the kind of property which gave them economic power, and therefore political power. The proletariat, on the other hand, possessed no power, only their own ability to work – *labour*. In Marx's view it was inevitable that the powerful capitalists would exploit the less powerful proletariat. A view that he expressed in one of his books was that the differences between the two main social classes (capitalists and proletariat) would continue to increase until they reached breaking point, and at this point in time a revolution would take place. This has not happened in England, and Marx has often been criticised for his wrong prediction. Where revolutions have taken place – Russia, China, Cuba, for example – they have been in rural, agricultural societies rather than capitalist economies.

However, most theorists about social class are very greatly indebted to Marx for his powerful analysis, even if his prediction has not been exactly fulfilled. It is also important to point out that although class was, for Marx, basically economic, he did not deny the importance of other social factors which permeated all aspects of life in society. Power, social prestige, and distinctive life-styles tended to make up a class sub-culture, but Marx saw the sub-structure to all this as being man's relationship to production, i.e. ownership or non-ownership of capital.

Money may be a pre-requisite, but . . .

[Source: *Andy Capp* no. 30 by Smythe (IPC)]

Max Weber

Many sociologists, including Max Weber, have suggested that Marx presented an over-simplified model of class structure. They have suggested that there are other aspects of class as well as the economic one, and that the economic aspect is not necessarily the most important. These theorists, basing their ideas on the work of Max Weber, have suggested three main aspects of class:

1 *economic* inequalities (essentially economic, but carrying with them social life-chances – *economic class*);
2 *status* inequalities, i.e. questions of social prestige, such as the consumption or spending of income and wealth and other aspects of life-style;
3 inequalities in *power*, that is, the ability to control others.

According to Weber, an individual's social standing *might* depend on his economic position, but the relationship may not necessarily be a direct one. In particular, Weber suggested that the way that individuals thought was *not* necessarily the same just because they did the same job. In particular Weber was interested in religious differences and the effect that this might have on thought processes, especially ambitions or aspirations, how people of differing religious beliefs viewed spending money, etc. Weber also suggested that how a person saw himself in relationship to the status system was as important, and perhaps more important, than his 'real' position. In more concrete terms, we can probably all think of individuals who 'objectively' would be working-class by any criteria, but who think of themselves as middle-class and, because of this, behave more like middle-class people in such matters as voting behaviour, dress, furniture, attitudes to education for their children, and so on.

Social Classification

To return to the three aspects of class (economic, status, and power), an individual's social position will tend to be about the same as judged by all three factors, but these positions may not necessarily match completely. A bookmaker might be high on income but low on social prestige and low on power. A retired general might be low on income but high in terms of social prestige. For many purposes the economic factor is a pre-requisite (without money you may be a non-starter), but it is not necessarily a guarantee of high general placement. But for many practical purposes, including many sociological surveys, this three-point division of social class is far too cumbersome. In practice, class is often judged by membership of an occupational group. This is how people have been classified in most social surveys, including surveys conducted for educational purposes, such as the Newsom Report and the Crowther Report, which were referred to in the last chapter. Many surveys rely on the Registrar General's classification of occupations, or simplified versions of it. This classification splits people up into five occupational groups:

1 professional and administrative (e.g. doctors, lawyers, top civil

servants, business executives)

II intermediate (e.g. the lesser professions, technical jobs, and less important business occupations)

III skilled $\begin{cases} \text{non-manual (e.g. typists, commercial travellers)} \\ \text{manual (e.g. electricians, plumbers, etc.)} \end{cases}$

IV semi-skilled manual workers (e.g. bus conductors, machine operators, etc.)

V unskilled manual workers (e.g. labourers, cleaners, road sweepers, etc.)

For sociologists, especially if they are interested in discussing the cause of social class or its effects on other aspects of social life, this is a very crude system of classification which ought to be described as a classification of occupational groups rather than a classification of five social classes. For analytical purposes, Social Class I is very unsatisfactory because it neglects the ownership of wealth, i.e. since it is based on occupation we get no idea of the number of extremely wealthy and powerful people, nor can we distinguish between these people (and their life-styles and life-chances) and professional people whose income and wealth is much less, such as doctors, lawyers, and university teachers. Class II is also unsatisfactory because it contains quite different social groups, some belonging to the minor administrative professional and managerial occupations and others who are the owners or managers of small shops and businesses. Class III is also open to criticism; for one thing, it includes more than half the male population. It consists mostly of skilled manual workers, but there are also a number of the lower ranks of the lower-middle-class occupations such as shop assistants and routine clerks, as well as foremen and supervisors. It is therefore too big and too mixed to be very useful in detailed sub-classifications.

However, despite these criticisms, this crude system of classification is useful, and it does have some kind of objective validity. There are measureable differences between one group and another. For example, infant mortality is much higher in Social Class V than in Social Class I (about 40 per 1000 compared with about 17 per 1000). Size of family is larger for Social Class V than it is for Social Class I. The height and weight of children differ from one group to another, and so on.

In other words, although this is a very crude system of classification, it does enable people to make generalisations about certain life-chances and certain aspects of life-style. This is probably because there is a very high correlation between occupation and income and educational background and other important variables. As we saw in the previous chapter, there is a great deal of evidence to show that children's performance in formal education is determined to some extent by social-class position.

The Hall–Jones Scale

Another system of occupational classification, which avoids some of the disadvantages of the Registrar General's classification, is the Hall–Jones scale. This is a seven-point scale:

I professional and high administrative,
II managerial and executive,
III inspectional, supervisory, and other non-manual higher grades,
IV inspectional, supervisory, and other non-manual lower grades,
V skilled manual and routine grades of non-manual,
VI semi-skilled manual,
VII unskilled manual.

Category I includes all occupations calling for highly specialised experience, possibly a degree or professional qualification needing long training. Category II includes those responsible for initiating policy, e.g. personnel managers or primary-school headmasters. Category III employees do not have so much responsibility but may have some authority over others, e.g. police inspectors and assistant teachers. In Category IV, authority over others is limited, but some responsibility is involved, e.g. costing clerks. Category V consists of skilled work which involves special training or an apprenticeship. In Category VI come jobs where no special skills or responsibility is involved but where the worker is doing a *particular* job habitually; whereas Category VII consists of unskilled work which requires no special training and is *general* in nature rather than associated with a particular industry.

Questions for Discussion

I

'Roles in Bushman society are founded upon sex, age and kinship. Some of the most important social distinctions derive from differences of sex. A man hunts and snares game, collecting any roots and fruits he may find while doing so; he prepares skins, making clothing for his family; he makes weapons, arrow poison, fire-sticks; he twists rope, manufactures the larger wooden vessels, makes fire, and occasionally helps the women in fetching wood and water. His wife builds the rough shelter for her family, cares for the children, gathers and prepares food, maintains the fire, makes her own ornaments, and is responsible for keeping the camp clean.
    The next important distinction is that of age. For a boy the great turning-point is the moment when he shoots his first buck. Paste is made from the animal's meat, and a row of scars is cut on his face,

arms and chest. Thereafter he is a man and is free to marry. A girl may be married when she is still a baby, but it is a marriage in name alone. Only when she is physically mature does she assume the roles of wife and married woman. Bushmen show respect for their old folk and obey their commands even though they may be invalids. When a man is old and a woman past the age of child-bearing they are free from the taboos which govern their juniors. They take up the less active roles of experts on traditional lore and family connexions. Cripples, invalids, and old people are looked after by their juniors.

Other obligations are fixed by the ties of kinship. The services performed by mothers and fathers in the upbringing of children are obviously of the most fundamental importance in the organization of the society. In later life they are replaced by another set of mutual obligations between the parents and their now adult sons or daughters. The relationship between husband and wife is strictly speaking one of affinity rather than kinship, but for present purposes affinal relationships may be grouped with kinship ones as principles defining the allocation of roles. A marriage is easily dissolved: a man can dismiss his wife or a woman go off with another man. But though divorce is so easy it hardly ever occurs, and married couples rarely quarrel with one another. Ties of kinship between bands are also important, for kinsfolk feel close together, and recognize an obligation to help one another when they can. Bushmen name their children after other members of their family but they are careful never to give a child the same name as his parent (Bushmen have no surnames). In this way there can be no confusion between the generations. Like peoples everywhere else they also avoid marriage between persons who are closely related, so that the ties of relationship are kept clear.

Distinctions of sex, age, and household grouping are all represented in the government of the bands, which is in practice the responsibility of the adult males. In the large bands they forgather every evening round the central camp fire, and, as the need arises, discuss what is to be done. They plan the following day's hunting, and periodically decide upon such other matters as moving camp or burning the veld to stimulate the growth of new plants. The council arranges trading and other visits to friendly neighbours. Unless the headman is an outstanding character, either because he has a gun or because he is a man of strong personality, he will have little authority over the other people. If a household is dissatisfied with his leadership of the band the members have only to leave and go to join some other group in which they have relatives. Indeed, the headman's power over his own household of one or two wives and their children is very limited and he may well be afraid of his wife's sharp tongue. The headman has no judicial functions; his hereditary privilege is to exercise control over the band's water supplies and veld food, but this is only a nominal duty and it does not matter if a boy of two or three years is the headman; elder kinsfolk can make the decisions for him. Thus it is not surprising that one author, when describing how the young heir to a vacant headmanship must wait until attaining maturity before assuming office, states that no regency is needed during his minority – things just go on. The important point is that the headman is also expected to act as leader, planning where the group will move and how it will conserve its resources. If the head-man is incompetent, senile, or an infant, someone else is recognized as leader. The study of the Kung Bushmen emphasizes that in such circumstances, rather than.choose the most intelligent hunter or man with the strongest personality for this role, the people simply take the man next in hereditary line. They do not reward him for accepting the extra responsibility; on the contrary, a leader is careful not to accumulate more possessions than other people for fear of exciting envy. "All you get is the blame if things go wrong", leaders say. No-one may stray far from the fixed pattern of sex, age, and kinship roles.'

[Source: *Roles* by M. Banton (Tavistock)]

a) To what extent do differences in sex determine roles in our society?
b) Which roles in our society are limited by age? Are these distinctions useful?
c) How important is kinship in our society?
d) What is the essential difference between leadership roles in Bushman society and in our society?
e) In what ways is a Bushman headman different from a British monarch?

2 A foreigner is puzzled by class distinctions in England. Clarify what we mean by class by saying something about each of the following questions.
a) How important is money?
b) How can I tell whether someone is working-class or middle-class? Do they wear different clothes?
c) Are these class differences enforced by law?
d) Can a working-class boy marry a middle-class girl? For example, could the son of a dustman marry a bank manager's daughter?
e) Can you move from one class to another? Down as well as up?

3 What did Marx mean by 'capitalist' and 'proletariat'? Do these two classes still exist in Britain today?

4 Weber talked about three aspects of class – *economic, status,* and *power*. Explain what each of them means.

Give an example of a person who might be wealthy but possess little prestige and power.

5
'In modern industrial life distinctions of sex, age and kinship remain of great importance in social organization, and though social strati-

fication has changed in character it has scarcely become any less significant. But the most striking development has been the increased specialization of social tasks and the diversification of society into hundreds of different sectors and subdivisions that seem to operate almost independently, following rules appropriate to them only. Consider the case of Enrico Francesci who opens a roadside cafe with the aid of his wife. He does the cooking and she serves the customers. His business prospers so that first he has to get a girl to help with the washing up, then another to assist in preparing the food. He has to start keeping accounts. The little restaurant becomes well known, so Mr Francesci builds a new dining room and takes on additional staff. No longer can he do the cooking himself. He employs a chef, a vegetable cook, a specialist in desserts, more kitchen hands and waitresses. He cannot run the restaurant as a family concern any longer. Whether he wishes to or not, Mr Francesci has to appoint supervisors, work out set menus, consult with the trade union leader over wages and conditions. Everyone's role has to be clearly defined to avoid friction, and the bigger the restaurant the more specialized these roles will be.

The more the concern grows the greater will be the difference between the earnings of the owner and the managers at the top, and the dish-washers at the bottom. Not many people have the temperament or the skill to manage a large organization, for it usually demands intelligence, an ability to take important decisions without getting nervous, self-confidence to go ahead with unpopular measures, and many other personal attributes apart from training and experience. Industrial societies therefore require highly complex incentives, selection procedures, and devices for removing or by-passing failures. The system has to go on working although people are being moved from place to place and up and down the social scale. These are only some of the things implied when such a social system is described as flexible by comparison with that of the Bushmen or of medieval Europe.

A big industrial concern must not be dependent upon the health or the memory of a single man. Everyone of importance must keep a record of his decisions so if something goes wrong one of his colleagues can consult the files and find out how matters stand. If a businessman orders some equipment he must know in advance what it will cost him. He must also know what taxes or customs duties he will have to pay on his deals, for otherwise he cannot calculate whether a transaction would be worthwhile. Business would come to a stop. All these rules and regulations mean a lot of paper work. The personal touch disappears and it no longer matters whether the recipient of a business letter can read the signature at the bottom provided he can see it has come from the proper office. Much as some people may deplore such things they are a logical and inevitable consequence of this form of social organization: the system has a logic of its own which necessitates certain policies irrespective of human will.'

[Source: *Roles* by M. Banton (Tavistock)]

a) 'Everyone's role has to be clearly defined to avoid friction. . . .'
   What does this mean? Can you give some examples?
b) If Enrico did not want to become a 'boss', how could he have avoided it?
c) It might be argued that Enrico 'got on' by his own (and his wife's) hard work. When he dies he might be a rich man. By what 'right' would his son inherit his money and business?
d) 'The system has a logic of its own which necessitates certain policies irrespective of human will'. This seems to suggest that the *system* is stronger than the *individuals* who make up the system. Do you agree?

Further Reading

Douglas, M. (ed.) *Man in Society*. Macdonald. (Chapter 4. 'Social Roles')
Worsley, P. (ed.) *Introducing Sociology*. Penguin. (Chapter 7. 'Social Stratification')
Beteille, A. (ed.) *Social Inequality*. Penguin

"I like your qualifications, Gribson – you have the makings of a first-class underling"

[Source: *Private Eye Cartoon Library 2* (cartoonist, Hector Breeze)]

8
Social Class
and Social Mobility

Social Mobility

One of the criticisms of Marx which is frequently made by non-Marxist sociologists is that his predictions have not come true. For example, they suggest that, far from the tendency for the differences in social classes becoming so great as to be intolerable and produce revolution, in fact there has been a trend in the opposite direction. What has tended to happen, they claim, is that there has been a 'filling-up of the middle', or a tendency for the working classes to move into middle-class positions and for there to be a much greater degree of fluidity in the social system. One of the key elements in this process, if it exists, would be a high degree of social mobility. But what evidence have we about the degree of social mobility in our society?

To what extent is it likely that individuals will move from one social class to another, or that their children will become members of a different social group from their own? First of all, in an expanding industrialised society there must be a certain amount of social mobility for two reasons: firstly because there tends to be an expansion of jobs at the top or in the middle and a contraction of jobs at the bottom – i.e. semi-skilled and unskilled manual work tends to disappear as industrialisation and automation proceeds. Secondly, there is a certain differential fertility in most industrial societies (including our own); that is, people in the higher social classes tend not to replace themselves in absolute numbers – in other words, married couples in Social Class I tend to produce an average number of children of less than two. So, in the United Kingdom, even if *all* children of Social Class I followed in their father's footsteps as far as class were concerned, there would still be some room at the top and therefore the need for some promotion from lower down the social scale.

This would be a fairly small amount of movement however. If we look at Table 11, from David Glass's book *Social Mobility in Britain*, we see that in fact less than half of the children born into Social Class I 'stay where they are', so this leaves even more room at the top.

Table 12
Sons' Occupations in Relation to Fathers' Occupations (Men, aged 21 and over, England and Wales, 1949)

Fathers' occupation	Sons' occupation							
	I %	II %	III %	IV %	V %	VI %	VII %	
Group I	38·8	14·6	20·2	6·2	14·0	4·7	1·5	(100)
Group II	10·7	26·7	22·7	12·0	20·6	5·3	2·0	(100)
Group III	3·5	10·1	18·8	19·1	35·7	6·7	6·1	(100)
Group IV	2·1	3·9	11·2	21·2	43·0	12·4	6·2	(100)
Group V	0·9	2·4	7·5	12·3	47·3	17·1	12·5	(100)
Group VI	0·0	1·3	4·1	8·8	39·1	31·2	15·5	(100)
Group VII	0·0	0·8	3·6	8·3	36·4	23·5	27·4	(100)

Note: The underlined figures show the proportions of sons of fathers in given occupational groups who had the same kind of occupation as their fathers.
[Source: *Social Mobility in Britain* by D. Glass (Routledge and Kegan Paul)]

The general picture presented by these figures is a long way away from 'perfect mobility' or 'random mobility', though. The chances of an unskilled or semi-skilled worker's son reaching Social Class I are very low indeed. It is still very much the case in our society that, for someone to become a member of Social Class I, the best qualification is to be the son of a Social Class I father. Further analysis of the above social-mobility table would reveal the following.

1 There is a great deal of *short-range* movement, for example, movement from unskilled to semi-skilled jobs, but much less mobility into the clerical, administrative, and professional ranks. The same applies to downward mobility: it is relatively uncommon for the sons of Social Class I parents to become semi-skilled or unskilled manual workers, although it is fairly common for them to drop down one or two classes.
2 In none of the seven categories was the *majority* of sons in the same category as their father, but in many cases the percentage was very high (especially Social Class V).
3 The greatest amount of inter-change is between sons of manual workers and the lower ranks of non-manual workers, and vice versa.
4 There is a greater degree of self-recruitment (i.e. of sons following their fathers) in the higher classes than in the lower. What the Table does not show is the proportion of all jobs which different occupational strata represent. Thus the fact that 38·8% of Class I sons followed their fathers and became Class I is in fact thirteen times greater than random-mobility chance, but for the sons of Class V fathers the figure of 47·3% is only slightly above chance.

The relation between social class and educational achievement has frequently been documented:

Table 13
Highest educational qualification achieved by British males, by social class.

	Social Class						
	I	II	III	IV	V	VI	All
Percentage in each class receiving:							
Degree or equivalent	53	8	7	0·3	0·1	0·2	5
Higher education below degree	20	10	12	2	0·5	—	5
G.C.E. A level or equivalent	10	9	10	4	2	1	6
G.C.E. O level or equivalent	7	20	20	12	6	3	13
C.S.E. below grade 1/commercial/apprenticeship	1	8	8	16	7	4	10
Foreign and other	5	4	4	3	3	1	3
None	3	41	39	63	81	90	57

[Source: *Social Class Differences in Britain*, by Ivan Reid (Open Books Publishing Limited, 1977)]

What cannot be derived from these figures is an answer to the question, 'To what extent is lack of mobility due to lack of ability?' In order to answer this we would have to have figures broken down for intelligence-test results. However, the figures given in Table 14, from the Robbins Report, give us some indication of what does happen.

Table 14
Highest course of education entered by children from maintained grammar schools by IQ at 11+ and father's occupation. GB Children born in 1940/1

IQ	Father's occupation	Higher education			'A' level	Other post-school course or 'O' level	No post-school course nor 'O' level	All children
		Full-time		Part-time				
		Degree-level	Other					
130 and over	Non-manual	37	4	10	7	41	—	100
	Manual	18	12	10	14	45	1	100
115–129	Non-manual	17	17	4	17	41	3	100
	Manual	8	7	9	10	53	13	100
100–114	Non-manual	6	11	8	7	64	4	100
	Manual	2	4	7	6	50	31	100

[Source: Table 4, *The Demand for Places in Higher Education*, 'The Robbins Report' Appendix 1 (HMSO)]

Since the 1944 Education Act, there has been an expansion of places in higher education, but this has not resulted in a greater proportion of university places being taken up by working-class students. It is also impossible to say at this stage exactly how important a part is played by education in determining mobility. Some writers have suggested that the most important factor is the occupational structure itself – especially the degree of industrialisation reached by the society – in other words the *overall amount* of general mobility is fixed by economic requirements, but the *range of mobility* may be connected with the educational system. Thus the *total* amount of social mobility is roughly the same in the UK, the USA and other Western European industrial countries, but the amount of long-range mobility (for example, the chances of an unskilled worker's son becoming a professional worker) is slightly greater in the USA because of differences in their educational system compared with ours: in the USA a larger percentage of all classes go to college, and admission to top jobs tends to be more formalised – i.e. paper qualifications are demanded.

Certainly the statistics given above do not support the exaggerated views of those who suggest that social class today is no barrier to educational or occupational success. In fact, although there has been some expansion of educational opportunity at secondary-school level, this does not in itself ensure overall social mobility. At the university level, professional and other middle-class groups are the ones most likely to take advantage of expansion of places. In occupational terms, there is no reason to believe that there is much more social mobility now than there was at the end of the nineteenth century. As we saw at the beginning of this discussion on social class, an essential characteristic of social class is that society is 'open' in the sense that it is possible to move from one group to another; but what is in dispute is the *extent* to which it is easier to move from one group to another now than it was say fifty or a hundred years ago. The evidence is that there has not been as much increase in social mobility as is popularly supposed. A particularly important point to be made is the distinction between long-range and short-range mobility; the Table from Glass's book on social mobility shows quite clearly that long-range mobility, i.e. moving from the top to the bottom or the bottom to the top, is still very rare indeed in our society.

The Distribution of Income and Property

Another popularly held belief is that in recent years, and especially since the war, there has been a steady process of evening out of wealth – that distribution of income and ownership of property have been made more equal and fair. It is sometimes suggested that the very rich and the very poor have disappeared, or are disappearing, and that we are now all somewhere near the average – some earning a little bit more than average, some a little less; some having more property, some less; but big differences being rare and not really very important. How true is this belief? What is the evidence?

The evidence most frequently produced to support this view concerns taxation policy since the war. There have been high rates of income tax designed to take money away from those earning high salaries and redistribute it to the most needy in society. There have also been passed such measures as death duties at a high rate which are designed to tax the inheritance of vast quantities of wealth and property from one generation to the next. So with these two kinds of policy it would seem obvious that the rich have got less rich and at the other end of the scale the poor have been given some of the wealth collected from the rich. *But does this happen in practice?* The answer seems to be that it is much more difficult to collect money from the rich than it would appear to be, and much more is involved than straight-forward taxation policy.

Official statistics are very helpful, especially those showing the distribution of personal incomes before and after tax, but nearly all the official publications in which these statistics are published contain advice about interpreting the statistics with very great care. The two great disadvantages about any official statistics (especially those derived from income-tax returns) is that very low incomes are generally excluded, and that, since the Tables refer to personal *income*, the amount of private *wealth* possessed by individuals is not contained. Many people are unaware of the fact that a sizeable proportion of the population have no need to work in order to produce an income, but can rely on their interest and capital gains. Although the official statistics do show that there are still considerable differences between the earnings of people in one occupation and another (and, despite the efforts of trade unions in the post-war years, the manual occupations still generally lag behind the non-manual occupations), it is still very important to stress when we are talking about income and *wealth* that the more serious inequality in our society is not inequality of earnings or inequality between occupational groups, but inequality in the possession of property – for example, valuable land which can be sold for building, capital in the form of factories or plant, and, of course, stocks and shares.

In the official taxation statistics, the wealth of very rich people does not appear at all, and someone who is a very wealthy owner of property may simply appear as a director of a company. In Britain in the mid-1950's it was estimated that two fifths of all private property was owned by only 1% of the adult population; and that four fifths (80%) was owned by only 10% of the population. It was shown that this was an 'improvement' on the situation at the turn of the century and, although the improvement has apparently continued since then (see Table 16, from *Social Trends* 1972), the real position is unclear since there is some suspicion that, in order to avoid taxes and death duties, precautions have been taken by the very wealthy to distribute their property among other members of their family and to take other kinds of evasive action.

101

Even so, the fact that the 1970 official statistics showed that the most wealthy 10% of the population still owned more than half of the country's wealth did cause a good deal of comment when it appeared in *Social Trends* 1972.

Table 15
The Changing Distribution of Personal Wealth in Britain

Stratum of the population	% of total net capital owned			
	1911–13	1924–30	1936	1951–6
Top 1%	65	59·5	56	46
Top 5%	86	82·5	81	67
Top 10%	90	89·5	88	79
Top 20%	—	96·0	94	89

[Source: H. F. Lydall and D. Tipping (Oxford University Bulletin of Statistics)]

Table 16
Distribution of Wealth by Groups of Owners (UK)

	1961	1966	1971	1974	1975	1976
Percentage of wealth owned by[1]:						
Most wealthy 1 per cent	28	24	20	18	17	17
Most wealthy 2 per cent	37	31	28	25	24	23
Most wealthy 5 per cent	51	44	41	37	35	35
Most wealthy 10 per cent	62	56	52	49	47	47
Most wealthy 25 per cent	79	75	72	71	70	68
Most wealthy 50 per cent	93	91	90	90	90	88
Total wealth (£ thousand million)	55	77	113	157	190	204

([1] rounded to nearest whole figure, hence percentages may not always total 100%)

[Source: *Social Trends* 1972, 1973 and 1979 (HMSO)]

It was also estimated that 80% of share capital is held by roughly 1% of the adult population. The efforts to redistribute wealth from the rich to the less rich by means of death duties have not been a great success. Death duties have become almost a 'voluntary' tax, in as much as it is quite possible legally to avoid paying death duties by various gifts and covenants. Similarly, although income tax is high, the most highly paid directors supplement their 'salary' by expense accounts and

Table 17
Distribution of Income after Taxation by Groups of the Population (UK)

	1961–63	1971–73
Percentage of income received by:		
Top 10 per cent	23·5	23·4
11–20 per cent	15·2	15·5
21–30 per cent	12·8	12·9
31–40 per cent	11·1	11·1
41–50 per cent	9·8	9·6
51–60 per cent	8·5	8·3
61–70 per cent	7·2	6·9
71–80 per cent	5·9	5·5
81–90 per cent	4·2	4·2
91–100 per cent	1·8	2·6

[Source: adapted from Table 24, Royal Commission on the Distribution of Income and Wealth, *Initial Report on the Standing Reference*, Cmnd 6171, July 1975 (HMSO)]

concealed income of various kinds such as cars and houses. Most of this avoidance of tax payment is strictly speaking quite legal and seems to be very difficult to overcome when, as one writer has put it, it means pitting the wits of an over-worked tax officer against very clever and highly paid accountants and solicitors.

Is England Still a Class Society?

One view put forward, not often by sociologists, but very frequently by politicians and journalists, is that the process of mixing up the social classes has become so great that it is no longer useful to talk in terms of class conflict, class consciousness, or even of a class society. This view is based on a number of factors: first of all the higher wages and higher standard of living of many of the working classes; secondly the narrowing gap which has *supposedly* taken place between the wages and standard of living of the working classes and of the middle classes; and also the fact that now working-class people are said to have similar tastes to middle-class people and differences in such things as voting behaviour are said to have become less marked. A similar argument is put forward to support the view that we are no longer a capitalist society, and some writers have written about 'the post-capitalist society'. The argument here is that, in the early days of capitalism, the capitalist, i.e. the person who owned the means of production such as the factory, was also in direct control of production; he was not only the owner, he was the owner/manager. It is now argued that most big industries are not personally owned, or even family owned, but are joint-stock companies, owned by the shareholders and managed by a new class of men who are not the owners but a professional group of technically minded managers. It is argued that, because of this change, these managers are no longer 'exploiters' in the sense that the capitalist owner/managers exploited their workmen, and that the new managing class is more likely to bear in mind the general social good of the country and questions of long-term growth rather than short-term profits.

However, the evidence in support of each of these four suggestions is conspicuously lacking. First of all, the idea that the working-class now receive higher wages and a high standard of living is true up to a point – namely, that union action has resulted in higher wages – but it is not true to say that differences have disappeared. It was pointed out in the section above that there have been very many ways of the better-off in society hanging on to their advantages. It is also probably true that generally the elderly working class in the population are still very badly off compared with the retired middle-class section of the community. The second point, that there has been a narrowing of the gap between working-class and middle-class people and that there is no longer any barrier between the classes, does not stand up to close investigation. Detailed studies of the Luton car workers, for example, show that there is considerable inter-mixing of the upper-working-class group with the lowest level of clerical workers but that inter-change does not go much further, and this does not necessarily bring with it changes in class consciousness or attitudes. This is related to the third point made; that is, that working-class tastes have become more bourgeois – what has sometimes been described as the 'em-bourgeoisement thesis'. The theory is that, as working-class people become rather more affluent, and as they are exposed to more middle-class 'culture' by means of television etc., their class loyalties and class consciousness cease to exist or to be so important, and the working-class tendency to vote Labour, for example, will diminish. Once again the evidence simply does not support this point of view. Admittedly, working-class people do adopt certain middle-class tastes, such as ownership of cars and holidays, but these are not really the most important class symbols. This tendency is simply a question of more people now being able to afford certain goods which previously were only within the grasp of the middle classes. As we shall see in a later chapter, there is no evidence to support the view that working-class people have become more bourgeois in their political outlook.

Finally, let us consider the view that class is less important because we are now living in a post-capitalist society where conflict has ceased to be a feature. First of all, the recent increase in the incidence of industrial disputes and strikes does not support this view of a harmon-ious classless society, and once again it would be the responsibility of those who put forward this thesis to produce the data to support it; so far, evidence is conspicuously absent. We can say, meanwhile, that there is no reason to assume that a professional group of managers would be any less capitalistic in their outlook than the old owner/managers. It has been shown, for example, that large numbers of the new pro-fessional manager group are owners in the sense that they receive quite large sums of money in the form of stocks and shares to supplement their income. Thus they have not only a professional interest in making sure that the company produces a profit (rather than good working conditions or high wages for the employees) but also a personal interest in valuing company profits rather than some more abstract quality in working conditions. It is also generally true that managers are not completely free agents, but have to work under the close scrutiny of directors; and in 1955 a paper in the Bulletin of Oxford Institute of Statistics showed that the directors of companies held shares on *average* worth £28 000 (by 1972 these shares would be worth about £60 000).

It is also true that the social background of the new managerial elite does not consist of workers who have somehow achieved promotion within the company. A number of studies (including Glennerster and Pryke, *The Public Schools*) showed that 64% of the executives of large British companies had been to public schools. The publication *The Director* in January 1963 also showed that over 75% of directors in the age group twenty-five to thirty-five years were ex-public school-boys, compared with the average for all age groups of 60%. This seems to show that if anything the ex-public-school group is tightening its hold on key positions in industry, rather than supporting the idea that industry is somehow becoming more open or democratic.

A different kind of evidence can be obtained from a variety of surveys about the importance of social class in England today. The work of John and Elizabeth Newson, for example (*Infant Care in an Urban Community*) shows that children grow up in very different physical and social environments according to their social class. A report by the National Child Development Study, *From Birth to Seven*, in 1972 gave a great deal of statistical evidence that social class was by no means insignificant in determining a child's 'life-chances'.

The Study found, for example, that the chances of an unskilled manual worker's child being a poor reader at seven-years old were six times greater than those of a child from Social Class I. The chances of an unskilled manual worker's child being a non-reader at age seven were fifteen times greater than those of a professional worker's child. More working-class children by this age were showing hostility to-wards teachers or were displaying withdrawal symptoms or depression and a tendency to write-off adult standards. As we have seen, the interpretation of these statistics is open to question, but what cannot be denied is that there is still a very close relationship between social class and behaviour in school.

Similarly, physical differences between children still correlate with social class. Children from Social Class I were on average found to be 1·3 inches taller than children from Social Class V. Families who most needed medical and welfare services were least likely to receive them. In Social Class I, only 1% of children did not go to the dentist, as against 31% in Class V. On questions of over-crowded housing and poor facilities, such as lack of in-door lavatory and bathroom, there were, in 1972, still tremendous social-class differences.

It used to be thought that if only we could have a Welfare State with free education then the differences between the classes would dissappear and we would be much nearer to a socially unified society where class was much less significant and where divisiveness was no longer a problem. Unfortunately this has not proved to be the case. For this purpose we can return once again to the evidence of hard data, namely infant-mortality rates divided into social-class groups (Table 18).

Table 18
Infant-mortality Rates per 1000 Legitimate Live Births by Social Class

Social Class	1921	1939	1950
I	38	27	18
II	55	34	22
III	77	44	28
IV	89	51	34
V	97	60	41
Average for all classes	79	47	29

[Source: Adapted from *Social Conditions in England and Wales as illustrated by Statistics* by A. M. Carr-Saunders, D. Caradog-Jones, and C. A. Moser, © 1958 Oxford University Press (by permission of The Clarendon Press, Oxford)]

In 1921 the infant-mortality rate for Social Class I (professional and managerial families) was 38 per 1000 compared with 97 per 1000 in Social Class V (unskilled manual workers). It was then thought that, if only medical services, including possibly a National Health Service, could be improved, then the gap would be narrowed by the figure for Social Class V gradually getting nearer to the figure of 38 per 1000 for Social Class I. In fact medical services were improved between 1921 and 1939, and after that time the National Health Service was introduced specifically to make medical services available to all sections of the community. As you can see from the Table 15, by 1950 the figure for the infant-mortality rates for Social Class V had got very close to what was the infant-mortality rate in 1921 for Social Class I; in that sense there was an improvement. *But*, by 1950 the infant-mortality rate for Social Class I had also been reduced, so that by that time the infant-mortality rate for babies of professional and administrative workers was very low indeed, namely 18 per 1000. In fact the clear picture that emerges from this is that, when improvements in services are provided, *everyone* benefits, irrespective of social class, and this has the side-effect of preserving the social-class difference; so the gap between Social Class I and Social Class V is as wide as ever, although all the figures have vastly improved since 1921.

Similar results can be seen by comparisons of university entrants in the 1920's and 1930's compared with the 1960's and 1970's. The overall number of places has increased (i.e. better opportunities are provided generally) but the *proportion* of working-class students getting places remains roughly the same (i.e. about 1·6% of the age group). So the lesson which is learned from such statistics as these is that, if we want to eliminate the differences caused by social-class background, whether in health or education, we have to do much more than provide 'equality of opportunity'. Real equality of opportunity is very difficult to achieve, and it is probable, that, if this is what we really want, we will have to embark upon a policy of 'positive discrimination' as suggested by the Plowden Report in 1963 – giving *better* facilities to the poor, rather than equal opportunities or worse opportunities, which is what still tends to happen in most cases.

Questions for Discussion and/or Written Work

1 'Britain is now a classless society, because it is quite possible for someone who is born poor to rise to positions of great wealth and importance.'

Sociologists might want to argue against this statement in at least two different ways.

a) What are the two kinds of argument?

b) Outline each of them in turn.

2 It is often assumed that death duties have reduced inequalities, but the evidence shows that this is not so:

'Why death duties have failed

Why have Britain's not inconsiderable taxes on capital failed to achieve any significant redistribution of wealth? Four reasons stand out:

1. Death duties are readily avoidable simply by transferring wealth by gifts.

2. Even when death duties are effective, they may have little direct effect in increasing wealth at the bottom end of the scale. In general they simply enable the government to reduce, or rather to check the increase in, the national debt. And while this reduces the amount of wealth held by the upper wealth group, it does not directly increase the wealth held by the rest.

3. Government help to the lower income groups has not generally taken the form of adding to their wealth. Thus these groups have been given pension rights and national assistance rather than investments; and the right to live in council houses at subsidized rents rather than property. These and other benefits can logically be regarded as the equivalent of capital held in trust by the government for these groups. To some extent, therefore, the true wealth possessed by the lower wealth group is appreciably under-estimated owing to the special legal form it takes.

4. A fourth reason why the distribution of wealth has changed only marginally is to be found in the type of asset in which the wealth is held. Briefly, the rich do not only have more money; they also make it multiply faster. Thus cash and fixed-interest securities represent 45 per cent of the wealth of individuals with less than £10 000, and equity shares only 5 per cent. By contrast, equities represent 56 per

cent of the wealth of those with over £250 000, and cash and bonds only 22 per cent. As a result, the average capital appreciation of the assets held by the wealthiest group, on this average composition, has been 114 per cent between 1950 and 1964; while the assets of the £3000–£10 000 group have appreciated by only 48 per cent.'

[Source: *The Economist*, 15 January 1966; reproduced in *Power in Britain*, ed. J. Urry and J. Wakeford (Heinemann Educational)]

a) What are death duties?
b) Why would it help if gifts were taxed?
c) What happens to the money collected in death duties?
d) It is suggested that the really important cause of inequality is not that some people *earn* more than others, but that some people own more *wealth* than others. What is meant by 'wealth' in this context?
e) Why is it that the rich tend to get richer?

3

'About forty company directors headed by Sir John Ellerman and Sir Harry Pilkington hold shares worth approaching £400m; as many as ten of Britain's largest and best known companies are under the effective control of a single family group; Britain's leading families who created companies like Pilkington, The Thomson Organization and Marks and Spencer each control wealth running into tens of millions of pounds. These are some of the conclusions of a pioneering study carried out by *Business News*.'

[Source: 'The £400M League' *Times Business News*, 15 December 1967; reproduced in *Power in Britain*, ed. J. Urry and J. Wakeford (Heinemann Educational)]

a) Why are sociologists interested in facts about income and wealth?
b) We often get the impression from newspapers that there are very few rich people left in this country. Discuss this view.
c) Does it really matter that some people in our society are very rich and others are very poor? Is this a sociological question?

4

'By and large, government in Britain has been concerned with maintaining finance capital and its capitalist basis. It accepts it as axiomatic that the Big Five Banks, ICI, and the oil companies are vital to Britain and that their interests are basically the interests of the nation ... The nationalization of coal, power, road and rail transport and steel was brought about by a compound of economic necessity and working-class pressure. Finance capital, however, was well able to adapt the newly nationalized industries to serve its interests, and then to mutilate them when it arrived at a position to make changes. A striking example of the interests of big finance-capitalist groups being fostered by State policy is given by the way in which the nationalized coal industry has been cut back, to the benefit of oil interests, and, again connected with this, by the atomic energy programme.

In the first years after the war there was a continual shortage of fuel. The National Coal Board's development programme was not yet bearing fruit, though the decline in the industry had been arrested and improvements in output per manshift and in recruitment were beginning to show. Even so, the Labour government's estimate of the future output of coal was extremely pessimistic, even while the Minister exhorted miners to put their backs into coal production. It was assumed that coal output would not rise beyond 200 million tons a year and would therefore inevitably fail to meet the needs of an expanding economy. The Conservative Party argued that, in any case, any real improvement in coal output demanded "sanctions" against the miners. Into this climate entered the predicted increase in the demand for oil for transport, steel-making and the like. The outcome was the Labour government's full encouragement to the oil companies in setting up refineries in Britain. Mr. Attlee was entirely justified in claiming that Stanlow, Fawley, Isle of Grain, Shellhaven and Coryton, representing the investment of hundreds of millions of pounds by the great Anglo-Dutch-American oil monopolies, could not have come into being without the initiative and active participation of the government. This was a major success for the oil monopolies.

Once in being, these great refineries had to find outlets for *all* their products – not only for the highly refined motor fuels and lubricants that would otherwise have been imported, but also for the residues, including the bunker fuels that could replace only coal. Naturally enterprises as aggressive as the oil monopolies, having got a foot in the door, proceeded to kick it open. Oil was offered to fill any gap between supply and demand for home-produced fuels. A period of intensive pressure and negotiation led finally to the announcement in 1955 of the privately owned oil monopolies' victory over nationalized coal. The government and ministries, the National Coal Board and the Electricity Board were all involved in the decision to expand rapidly the use of oil at power stations, with the aim by 1960 of burning five and two-thirds million tons a year, equivalent in heating value to nine million tons of coal. On this basis the State considered the economy secure against fuel shortage and at the same time had a powerful means of pressure on the miners. The way began to be opened for a new assessment of the National Coal Board's development plans in purely big-business terms.

In 1956, the consequences of invading Egypt revealed overnight the flimsy basis for the government's policy, and the gap between supply and demand for fuel gaped wide open again. It became clear that the power stations could hardly secure annually more than four and a half million tons of oil, equivalent to seven million tons of coal. But though the supply of oil had turned out to be insecure, the nationalized coal industry had still no opportunity to flourish. Influential interests came forward with the promise of a new power source, safe from the strength of the miners or of Arab nationalists.

[Source: *The Ruling Class* by S. Aaronovitch (Lawrence and Wishart); reproduced in *Power in Britain*, ed. J. Urry and J. Wakeford Heinemann Educational)]

a) What is meant by the 'ruling class' in this quotation?
b) If the 'ruling class' exist, would they be more likely to support or oppose nationalisation of oil companies? Why?
c) The author seems to approve of nationalisation but still criticises the Labour Party. Why?
d) Why are sociologists interested in topics which seem to be very 'political', for example, nationalisation, profits, power, etc.?

5
Table 19
Selected Differences in Terms and Conditions of Employment. Percentage of establishments in which the condition applies

	Factory workers	Clerical workers	Senior managers
	%	%	%
Holidays: 15 days +	38	74	88
Normal working 40+ hours per week	97	9	22
Pension – employers' scheme	67	90	96
Time off with pay for personal reasons	29	83	93
Pay deductions for any lateness	90	8	0
No clocking-on or booking-in	2	48	94

[Source: 'Workplace Inequality' by D. Wedderburn, *New Society*, London, 9 April 1970]

a) Which group appears to have the shortest working week?
b) Which of the three groups would you say (i) has the best working conditions, (ii) has the worst working conditions? Give brief reasons for your answer.
c) Why is it that the three groups of workers have different working conditions?
d) All three groups work, but which group would normally be classified as working-class? What is really meant by working-class?

Further Reading

Butterworth, E. and Weir, D. *The Sociology of Modern Britain*. Fontana. (Section 5)
Urry, J. and Wakeford, J. (eds) *Power in Britain*. Heinemann Educational Books

9
Work and Leisure

In industrialised societies, people tend to make a sharp distinction between work and leisure: in the English language we have two words in everyday use which people understand as being a contrast of some kind. This is not so everywhere: people living in pre-industrial societies tend not to make this distinction in their language and in their thinking. Why do we?

In simple societies, people certainly have to spend much of their time doing a number of things which use up a lot of their energy: for example, hunting or growing food, and protecting themselves from the weather. But this is not seen as *work* in the way that the word is used in England. The contrast we make between *work* and *leisure* is very largely a result of the Industrial Revolution. In a system where most people 'work for' someone else – an employer – the idea gradually develops of *'his* time' contrasted with *'my* time': in other words *work* and *non-work*, or work and leisure. The majority of adults in our society have to sell their labour for eight or nine hours a day in order to have the means to live when they 'clock-off'.

So, work as we know it today has been created by a certain kind of technology, and it is now a dominant influence in our culture. We have already seen in Chapter 7 that the job a person does, i.e. his occupation, may be a very useful way of predicting some aspects of his non-work behaviour – for example how he spends his money, his attitude to education, the age at which he thinks he ought to be getting married, the number of children he will produce, and so on. Why should there be this kind of relationship between work and non-work behaviour?

I have said that work tends to dominate our culture, and it is also true to say that it dominates individual adults and their children. A very large percentage of an adult's life is spent at work; it would be very surprising if what he or she did for eight or nine hours a day had no effect at all on his personality, his attitudes, or even his physical appearance. As we have already seen in an earlier chapter, Marx regarded a man's relationship to the means of production as basic to an understanding of his life. The economic system was the sub-structure or basic foundation; the rest of the culture was the super-structure (or building on top of the foundation) – and this was thought to be determined to a large extent (but not entirely) by economic factors. Marx thought that man's behaviour was not completely determined by his economic position, but it was considerably influenced by it. Marx saw the most important economic factor as a simple question of whether a man was the *exploiter* (i.e. the capitalist or bourgeois entrepreneur) or the exploited (i.e. the worker or proletariat); more recent sociological studies have tended to look at specific occupational differences rather than simple class contrasts, for example, the characteristics of miners or deep-sea fishermen as contrasted with those of bank clerks or insurance workers.

What is Work?

In our society, work is a specialised activity normally marked off from other activities by time and space; that is, work is usually undertaken for a specific period of time in a place away from home. So, if during my spare time I decorate my house, this is not work; but if I employ a painter to decorate it, the same task would be work for him. Most people watching a professional football match on a Saturday afternoon will be enjoying their leisure time; but a few will be working – for example a newspaper reporter who has to write an account of the match, or the team-managers and trainers who will also be at work. In other words, the same activity may be work for some and a leisure pastime for others. Many of the activities on which we spend our leisure time, such as sport, use up a great deal of energy; others, such as fishing or gardening, would be necessary activities in a primitive society but in our society have become leisure pursuits.

Why Work?

One simple, straight-forward answer is that most people work because they have to. They need the money to provide necessities for themselves and perhaps their families. But this is not the whole answer: our society places a particular importance and value on work. In the past this attitude to work had religious significance, and the tradition of valuing work and condemning 'idleness' and 'laziness' has survived to a large extent. The sixteenth-century and seventeenth-century puritans regarded work as an opportunity to demonstrate their worthiness, not only to their fellow men but to God. The successful, hardworking man was thought to be favoured by God – his success was a sign of God's grace – poor work was an insult to God; idleness was self-indulgence. This attitude continued into the nineteenth century and even to the beginning of the twentieth century: studies of unemployed men have shown them not only to be miserable at having no work to do, but also sometimes feeling 'guilty', even when they could not possibly be blamed for their lack of employment.

It may not only be a hangover from the puritan ethic which makes people want to work, however. Much work is a social, co-operative activity which seems to give a great deal of satisfaction to human beings. According to some sociologists, one of the tragedies of industrial society is the fact that what ought to be one of man's greatest and most enjoyable activities – co-operating with others in order to improve humanity's control of the environment – has become *exploitation*: most men do not work *with* each other but *for* someone else.

Today it seems to be true that only a minority of people really enjoy their work. Artists, independent craftsmen, professional workers, including some teachers, and some other groups may derive a great deal of pleasure from their work; but for the majority it is more likely that they feel *alienation*, that is, they regard work as something they have to do but which is an activity they do not really identify with – it lacks meaning for them. They work in order to be able to 'live' outside work.

Another reason for this kind of alienation felt by workers is the division of labour in industry. In factory production, most jobs have been reduced to a few very simple movements which require little skill, give less satisfaction, and have little meaning for the worker compared with the interest that a craftsman had in producing a complete object by himself. For many factory workers, such as those employed in car manufacturing, who have been studied intensively (see *The Affluent Worker* by Goldthorpe, Lockwood, Bechofer, and Platt), work becomes purely *instrumental*, that is, it becomes a means of enjoying real life in non-work time, rather than an enjoyable and meaningful activity in its own right.

R. Blauner has discussed the idea of alienation in a book called *Alienation and Freedom: the Manual Worker in Industry* (1963). Blauner talks of four kinds of alienation. One aspect is *'powerlessness'*, which he defines as the inability of the worker to have any control over his work – the worker has no influence over management decisions, and no control over conditions of employment or the immediate work processes such as the timing of jobs. Frequently opportunities are missed of consulting workers who could improve the product or the process; the workers see this and are frustrated by it. Blauner's second kind of alienation is *'meaninglessness'*; this is the inability of the worker to have any sense of purpose in the work situation, because it is difficult to see the relationship between the job the worker is doing and the overall production process – each worker only does his little bit, and no attempt is made to relate this small task with what is being produced ultimately. The third dimension of alienation is *'isolation'*; this is the lack of a feeling of belonging or of membership in industrial communities. This results in a very impersonal administration and also the absence in large factories of informal groups – i.e. workers tend to be treated as if they were bits of isolated machinery rather than human beings who have normal friendship patterns when they are at work. Workers are still referred to as 'hands' in many factories! The fourth dimension suggested by Blauner is *'self-estrangement'*, which indicates the impossibility of the worker becoming really involved in work as a means of self-expression. This is the result of work being separated from the rest of the worker's social life and of work becoming simply instrumental – that is, a source of income – rather than being a satisfying, co-operative, or even aesthetic experience.

Work and Society

Another interesting fact about work in our society is that not all work is equally valued by society. Some kinds of work appear to merit high prestige and high rewards, other kinds of jobs low prestige and rewards. The strange fact is that some of the low-prestige jobs in our society, such as those of dustmen and sewerage workers, are much more useful than supposedly high-prestige jobs such as advertising managers or salesmen. Many kinds of societies have to persuade some people to do low-prestige work for low rewards, while they see others doing 'better' jobs for more money. How is this persuasion successful? One extreme solution is to remove choice from the situation – that is, by employing slave labour. This was practised in the West Indies and the southern states of America, where the hardest jobs were done by people who were not free to leave and move on. Another solution is to have a caste system which is justified by religion: low-status workers 'learn' that it is the will of God that they should accept their lot in life. Yet another possibility is the present South African method which defines black people as inferior and therefore capable of only certain low-status jobs and legally kept out of certain other jobs which are better paid and which carry higher prestige. In nineteenth-century England, workers were persuaded to do very unpleasant work for low rewards because their bargaining power was deliberately kept low. The factory owners at that time were supported by the law, the police, and, when necessary, the army; while the workers were denied even the legal right to trade unions or collective bargaining by such legislation as the Combination

Acts. It was, therefore, a very uneven struggle, and workers were forced to accept their low pay and status or starve. Even today, when trade unions are legal, the wages of many unskilled workers are still low: how is this achieved? One technique is to persuade people to accept the argument that skill and intelligence *should* be rewarded. This is a widely accepted view in our society, but it is very difficult to justify logically. Another device is to make sure that, in a society where skill and training are rewarded, access to such skills and training is made much easier for some people than for others. But this 'inequality' is disguised as much as possible. A final technique, referred to in a previous chapter, is to disguise high earnings by calling them something else – an expense account, or having 'perks' such as free company cars plus running costs (tax free). In all cases the low-paid workers have to be 'socialised' into thinking that the existing state of affairs is 'right' or 'natural' or a matter of luck. Jeremy Tunstall in an interesting book called *The Fishermen* (1962), about Hull deep-sea fishermen, gives an example of such socialisation. He shows that most boys who become deep-sea fishermen in Hull come from the lower streams of the secondary-modern schools near the docks. At these schools the boys have been socialised to see themselves as inevitably becoming un-skilled manual workers; they also see the teacher as a representative of the white-collar privileged workers. Fishing is seen as an escape into the world of real men, a world in which, because it is a closed community, they will not be looked down upon by superior people.

We should not, of course, assume that all men who are manual workers dislike their jobs and that all non-manual workers get high satisfaction out of their position. Manual workers differ considerably from one industry to another (as well as from one individual to another). Some manual work still retains elements of craftsmanship; for example, one study of the printing trade showed that only 4% of printers were dissatisfied with their jobs, whereas 61% of car workers were dis-satisfied. This fits in with the kind of alienation pattern suggested by Blauner above. In the car industry, workers tend to be totally dominated by the machine. It may also be true though that clerical jobs are becoming more routine and more limited in their promotion prospects – it is probably harder to work your way from a minor clerical position to management now than it was in pre-war years. Alienation may therefore become a serious feature of clerical work, rather than being confined to manual jobs in industry.

Automation

The two significant features of the Industrial Revolution were the increased use of *mechanisation* and the division of labour. Jobs which had been done by manual labour were taken over by machinery, and also jobs which had been undertaken by one individual worker were split down into a series of much smaller tasks. This speeded up production and reduced prices of manufactured goods, but it did have a number of side-effects, especially the kind of alienation which has already been mentioned.

The process of division of labour and mechanisation – i.e. industrialisation – is, however, quite different from the process of *automation*. 'Automation' is the name given to industrial processes which use machinery and computers not only to make the goods but also to control, by 'feedback' mechanisms, the rate of production, the input of raw materials, and the co-ordination of separate processes. In automated factories less manpower is needed, but workers have to understand the whole process, and their responsibility is much greater. Thus in some senses automation is a reversion to the state of affairs where individual workers had to understand the whole process; it should therefore be seen as quite distinct from mechanisation or industrialisation. It is often suggested that the process of automation is going to change industrial society completely. There are certainly reasons for optimism if automation could be used to release workers from routine jobs and if working conditions could thus become more human; but, automation is proceeding comparatively slowly, and it is unlikely that automation can be used in most industrial situations. A very large plant is required to 'justify' the expense of automation. So long as the factory owners and management are concerned with profits rather than with the quality of life of their workers, it is extremely unlikely that automation will solve all the problems of alienation in society.

Leisure

What is leisure? I have already made the distinction between work and non-work, but leisure is not the same as non-work. The category of non-work time is self-explanatory, but leisure forms only part of non-work time. Non-work time also includes essential functions such as eating and sleeping; the time left over after these essential functions may be termed leisure.

Since the emergence of the concept of leisure, certain interesting changes have taken place. To begin with there were great disparities between the industrial working classes, who worked very long hours and had very little leisure time, and the 'leisured classes' who may not have worked at all. For this reason, leisure has strong social-class connections. Many leisure-time pursuits began as upper-class pastimes and have worked their way down the social scale. Others, such as football, began as rough working-class sports and have eventually become more respectable. Activities like archery and fencing began as the essential practical skills of warriors of various social grades and have only recently become sports with social-class connections.

Today there is less difference in the *amount* of leisure time available to different social classes. Most people now have a five-day week and an eight- or nine-hour day. There are still differences in length of annual holidays, so that white-collar and managerial workers still tend to enjoy longer vacations, but there seems to be a tendency for the social groups to get closer in this respect. But when we come to the question of how leisure time is spent, we shall see that there are still considerable differences connected with social class. This is partly a question of cost – some kinds of leisure pursuits are simply too expensive for working-class or even lower-middle-class people, playing polo is an example of this – but cost is not the whole explanation for differences in leisure pursuits. Many other factors are involved in leisure. For example, Howard Becker made a study of jazz musicians

117

and showed that the unusual hours of work common in this particular occupation had the effect of making their whole pattern of life abnormal. Becker suggested that it was the abnormal rhythm of life that accounted for their non-conformity in other respects. This is contrary to the 'commonsense' view that non-conformists become jazz musicians, rather than the other way round. Less dramatic examples are provided by working-class people who work shifts or continuous night work – this severely limits their leisure possibilities. There are a great number of studies of social class, or occupational position, with leisure pursuits, and some of these will be considered below.

How Much Leisure?

We know from many historical documents that in the nineteenth century the average working week for a factory worker was at least seventy hours a week for fifty-two weeks in the year. This has now been reduced to something like forty-four hours a week. But, before jumping to the conclusion that such progress is steady and inevitable, we should note that the amount of work expected today is probably much more than the workload of the typical peasant in the Middle Ages who perhaps worked as little as 194 days a year, owing to the great number of religious feast days which were regarded as holidays. (The word 'holiday' is of course a corruption of 'holy day'.) There is no reason why we should regard a forty-hour week or even a thirty-five-hour week as 'normal' in any meaningful sense.

It is often suggested that high levels of industrialisation, and especially automation, will reduce the number of working hours and therefore increase the amount of leisure time. The evidence on this is, however, not so optimistic. The average working week for manual workers in 1938 was forty-eight hours, and by 1968 this had only dropped to forty-six hours. Today there is a great deal of overtime worked which puts the average working week up above the minimum, or the trade-union week, of five days of eight or nine hours a day. It is also quite common for people to take second jobs, and this kind of 'moonlighting' also increases the average working week of a large proportion of the population. In 1964 a Gallup-poll survey showed that one out of every six men had a spare-time job which took up an average of twelve hours a week out of his potential leisure time. Workers in Britain are also out of step with those of many other industrial societies. In America, for example, the normal working year is 1976 hours, compared with the average of 2137 hours in Great Britain. The idea that we are rapidly moving towards a time when most people will have vastly increased amounts of leisure time at their disposal does not stand up to close scrutiny. We may be gradually moving in this direction, but it is unlikely that any dramatic change will occur in the near future.

How Is Leisure Time Spent?

For all social classes, most leisure time is spent at home with other members of the family. Much of the evidence which we have about how leisure is spend in England is derived from BBC surveys of leisure pursuits including radio and television watching. We know that during the week over 70% of adults are at home between 8 p.m. and 10 p.m. Over the weekend the figure falls to about 60%. Despite some variations of sex and age and class, spending leisure at home is 'normal' for all sections of a community. Again for all sections of the community, the main leisure activity at home is watching television. The average viewing time for adults is about seventeen hours a week, and there are no serious social-class differences in this. Over 40% of the adult population is reckoned to be watching television at 9 o'clock in the evening on any typical weekday. But, beyond this basic time spent watching television, the results of BBC surveys show that the population spends the rest of its leisure time in a very wide variety of pursuits. For example, 22% said they were interested in classical music and 13% in ballet; but these are minority tastes, and the surprising result of such surveys is that they show the population to be split up into a large number of minority-interest groups. Differences in income naturally have a limiting effect. Family-expenditure surveys show that, as we would expect, the more affluent members of the population spend more money on restaurants, alcohol, travel, theatres, holidays, and sports goods. But this is hardly surprising; less well-off members of society spend money on much the same things, but have less of it to spend.

Leisure and Occupation

A number of studies have been undertaken comparing middle-class and working-class leisure time, and perhaps more usefully the difference between specific occupational groups. Generally, middle-class adults tend to belong to more clubs and associations than do working-class people. They also tend to be more active in the groups of which they are members. There is a slight tendency for more middle-class people to take their leisure pursuits outside the home. The BBC research has shown that on a typical weekday between 8.30 and 9 o'clock in the evening, 26% of the upper-middle-class group are outside the home compared with 20% of working-class adults engaged in leisure pursuits. Similarly, only 32% of the upper-middle-class group were watching television, compared with 46% of the working-class adults. Some writers have generalised such findings as these by saying that working-class people tend to spend their leisure time passively (either watching professional sport or just listening to broadcasts or watching television) whereas the middle classes tend to be more active in their leisure pursuits: meeting friends, joining clubs, playing sport, etc. There is a *tendency* in this direction, but the differences between social-class groups in this respect are comparatively *small* and should not be exaggerated.

The usual explanation for these small class differences is that manual occupations demand more in both time and energy, so that manual workers are more likely to want to relax physically in their leisure time rather than expend more energy playing sports, for example. There may well also be important educational differences which have significant effects on leisure activities. Middle-class workers are generally more highly educated than working-class adults, and as a result of education a certain amount of stimulation may have taken place to continue with certain pursuits in adult life. But the idea that all or even a sizeable proportion of the middle classes spend their leisure time actively or on creative pastimes is quite wrong. Other generalisations, such as that middle-class people tend to spend their time reading whereas working-class people watch television, are similarly complete distortions of the truth. Studies of differences between specific occupational groups are generally rather more fruitful than contrasts between working-class and middle-class behaviour.

For example, one study by Stanley Parker looked at the leisure pursuits of bank clerks, youth-employment officers, and child-care officers. Parker found that the youth-employment officers and child-care officers were more interested in their jobs and found them much more meaningful than the bank clerks. The bank clerks tended to look at leisure as being completely cut-off from work, and they used their leisure to complement or compensate for their dull routine job. On the other hand, the youth-employment officers and the child-care officers did not draw such a rigid line between work and leisure; they often used their spare time as an extension of their work, and they did not always find it easy to decide when they were working and when they were at leisure – they might be reading a book which they found interesting but which would also be useful in their job, or they might be talking to friends or colleagues about their work in a way which again could be useful. All three of these jobs were roughly equivalent in terms of status or prestige, but the effect of the type of work upon the three groups towards their leisure time was quite different. The importance of this kind of study is that it shows that the relationship between work and leisure is quite complex and is not simply a question of middle-class and working-class, or even of status levels within those groups: it is much more a question of involvement in work or seeing the meaning of the job which is involved.

Other studies of extreme patterns of working-class life show clearly the way in which the kind of work that a man does has a strong effect on his non-work behaviour. Studies of coal miners, for example, give us a picture of the coal-face worker who is deeply involved in his work, although he may hate it, and regards the danger as a test of his manliness. But the dangerous work does have the advantage of ensuring a co-operative team spirit between coal miners – they rely on each other to prevent death or serious accidents. This team spirit between groups of workers tends to be relived outside work – probably in the pub, especially during the weekend. Studies also show that men who do this kind of work, not necessarily in coal mines, expect their wives to spoil them and to play the role of servant rather than to be an equal partner in marriage; but most of this evidence is rather old, and the pattern may be changing.

Other studies, such as Tunstall's of deep-sea fishermen, also show that work spills over into leisure time and home life. Fishermen also have to do hard dangerous work which involves a good deal of co-operation. These teams of fishermen tend to spend their periods of leisure time ashore together. A difference here would be that their spending tends to be concentrated in a few days' shore leave. This may separate wives and husbands and exaggerate the differences in their roles: the Hull trawlermen expect their wives to play a servant's role rather than to join in leisure-time activities.

It should be remembered, however, that these are extreme examples. Some social-class differences have often been exaggerated or at least misrepresented and distorted. Some accounts of social class and England give quaint stereotypes of the beer-drinking working-class man on the one hand, who expects his wife to stay at home and wait for him, and the middle-class 'culture-seeking' couples who rarely watch television but spend their time reading books or going to the theatre or watching ballet and opera. These are crude and unhelpful stereotypes – most of the 'high-culture' pursuits mentioned are such minority tastes that it is misleading to think of them as in any sense middle-class pastimes.

Leisure and the Family: Age and Sex Differences

Most people spend the majority of their leisure time within the family group. Some studies have shown that wives usually have less leisure time than their husbands and that their range of leisure-time activities is less wide. This may be a misleading result however; wives often spend time in the home on activities where the borderline between work and leisure is difficult to draw. Many women would regard sewing as a leisure pusuit, but surveys might show this as work for mothers rather than as a pastime. Nevertheless, BBC audience research does show that between 8.30 p.m. and 9 p.m. 46% of men are watching television and another 22% are engaged in some leisure outside the home, but only 40% of women are watching television and 18% engaged in outside leisure activities. It may well be, then, that women tend to be more confined to the home, but the actual leisure-time differences between men and women are not very great. Men are also more often involved in political activities and tend to belong to more clubs, especially sporting clubs, and also go to pubs more often than women.

Sex differences in this respect appear long before marriage. Boys and girls tend to be socialised into different roles, and girls are generally brought up more strictly and supervised more closely by their parents. Girls, even when they are at work, are often expected to do more work around the house than their teenage brothers. This may have some effect on their real leisure time as well as the range of their activities.

As young people get older, their leisure time tends to change, as well as the patterns of their leisure-time behaviour. These age differences are much more significant than social-class or sex differences. Of particular importance in this respect is the group already referred to as 'adolescents'. Adolescents are the group with least attachment to the family as far as leisure is concerned. During adolescence, young people tend to drift away from the family to be much more involved in their peer group, to try out all sorts of new interests and activities. Adolescents are the group least interested in watching television and most interested in peer-group activities. They spend more time outside the home than any other age group: according to the BBC survey, on a typical weekday evening only 55% of the fifteen to twenty-four age group were at home between 8.30 p.m. and 9 p.m. (compared with 71% of the twenty-five to forty-four age group). The fifteen to twenty-four age group are the greatest frequenters of cinemas, dance-halls, and coffee bars. We have already examined in a previous chapter the question of youth culture and the commercial interest in this particular age group, but it seems very likely that young people will want to extend their range of interests, acquire new tastes, and meet more young people than will the more staid, older age groups. It is also this age group who show great interest in attending the theatre and going to parties, but also in classical music and travelling abroad. It is certainly a stereotype rather than a truth to think of all young people as being pop fans and spending their time in coffee bars and discotheques: the tastes of young people, as with older people, cover a very wide range indeed. However, it is generally true that, as people grow older, the range of their leisure interests and activities become more limited. This is partly the result of the end of the period of adolescent experimentation, but also a tendency for middle-aged people to settle down into a more definite way of life with more rigid tastes and life-patterns.

Finally, the older members of society, especially when they retire, might now be regarded as a problem group as regards leisure. This is a group of people who have, by definition, a great deal of leisure time at their disposal but who may not have a very wide range of interests and will usually have less money than the rest of the community. Once again, we have to be wary of journalistic exaggeration: several surveys have shown that only a minority of old people are really socially isolated or complain about loneliness. The majority of old people appear to withdraw from society voluntarily rather than of necessity, although the minority of poverty-striken retired people is certainly one of the unsolved problems of the Welfare State. But for most retired people there may be a shortage of really involving leisure-time pursuits, and a small number of retired people certainly are unhappy: more of them die soon after retirement than would be regarded as 'normal'. Education for retirement is a developing subject in many adult-education establishments.

The Future of Work and Leisure

I began this chapter by suggesting that work is a dominant influence in our culture. Some writers have suggested that domination by work will give way to domination by leisure. The argument is that in an age of automation work will become less and less significant, both as an economic divider between rich and poor and also as a prestige-giver. It is argued that it will be much more significant in the future to see people in terms of their leisure pursuits rather than their work connections.

I am rather sceptical of this view in its extreme form. For one thing, I have already suggested that it seems highly unlikely that automation will proceed as quickly or as completely as some have suggested. It seems probable that work will continue to dominate the lives of the vast majority of the population. Nevertheless, it is certainly true that the importance of leisure has increased considerably and is continuing to do so. Others have argued that workers in future will seek employment with one eye on the leisure facilities available either in that district or supplied by the firm itself. But this kind of situation is only likely to o ccur at a time of full employment, in other words when labour is scarce. One of the recent features of life in Great Britain has been the return of unemployment and the fear of unemployment. Under such conditions as these it seems unlikely that employers will devote too much of their space and other resources to recreational facilities for their workers. Leisure is certainly very different now from what it was even thirty or forty years ago, and people's attitudes to leisure have changed considerably, but to think of the present time or even the near future in terms of 'the age of leisure' seems to me to be a considerable exaggeration.

Questions for Discussion and/or Written Work

1 What do we mean by *'work'* and *'leisure'*? Why is the idea of *leisure* important in our society?

2 We have seen that the idea of *alienation* is a very complex one. The following extract from the writings of Karl Marx gives one aspect of alienation.

'In what does this alienation of labour consist? First, that the work is *external* to the worker, that it is not a part of his nature, that consequently he does not fulfil himself in this work but denies himself, has a feeling of misery, not of well-being, does not develop freely a physical and mental energy, but is physically exhausted and mentally debased. The worker therefore feels himself at home only during his leisure, whereas at work he feels homeless. His work is not voluntary but imposed, *forced labour*. It is not the satisfaction of a need, but only a *means* for satisfying other needs. Its alien character is clearly shown by the fact that as soon as there is no physical or other compulsion it is avoided like the plague. Finally, the alienated character of work for the worker appears in the fact that it is not his work but for someone else, that in work he does not belong to himself but to another person.'

[Source: *Selected Writings in Sociology and Social Philosophy* by Karl Marx, ed. T. B. Bottomore and M. Rubel (Watts). Reproduced in *Sociological Theory, A Book of Readings*, ed. L. A. Coser and B. M. Rosenberg (Collier-Macmillan)]

a) Marx is talking about work in a nineteenth-century factory. Why is it suggested that the worker feels that work is a kind of misery?
b) Do you think that Marx might have enjoyed his own work – i.e. writing books? What was the essential difference between that kind of work and being a 'hand' in a factory?

c) In what sense was work in a nineteenth-century factory 'forced labour'?

d) Could factory work still be described as forced labour?

e) To what extent is the idea of alienation useful for describing certain aspects of life in modern industrial society?

3 One of the questions asked in this chapter was, 'How are some people in society persuaded to do hard, unpleasant work for less wages than those doing much more pleasant work?' The following extract is about the USA at the end of the nineteenth century.

'To be a Negro
James Weldon Johnson (1871–1938)

There were some black and brown boys and girls in the school, and several of them were in my class. One of the boys strongly attracted my attention from the first day I saw him. His face was as black as night, but shone as though it were polished; he had sparkling eyes, and when he opened his mouth, he displayed glistening white teeth. It struck me at once as appropriate to call him "Shiny Face", or "Shiny Eyes", or "Shiny Teeth", and I spoke of him often by one of these names to the other boys. These terms were finally merged into "Shiny", and to that name he answered good-naturedly during the balance of his public school days.

"Shiny" was considered without question to be the best speller, the best reader, the best penman – in a word, the best scholar, in the class. He was very quick to catch anything, but, nevertheless, studied hard; thus he possessed two powers very rarely combined in one boy. I saw him year after year, on up into the high school, win the majority of the prizes for punctuality, deportment, essay writing, and declamation. Yet it did not take me long to discover that, in spite of his standing as a scholar, he was in some way looked down upon.

The other black boys and girls were still more looked down upon. Some of the boys often spoke of them as "niggers". Sometimes on the way home from school a crowd would walk behind them repeating:

"Nigger, nigger, never die,
Black face and shiny eye."

On one such afternoon one of the black boys turned suddenly on his tormentors and hurled a slate; it struck one of the white boys in the mouth, cutting a slight gash in his lip. At sight of the blood the boy who had thrown the slate ran, and his companions quickly followed. We ran after them pelting them with stones until they separated in several directions. I was very much wrought up over the affair, and went home and told my mother how one of the "niggers" had struck a boy with a slate. I shall never forget how she turned on me. "Don't you ever use that word again", she said, "and don't you ever bother the coloured children at school. You ought to be ashamed of yourself." I did hang my head in shame, not because she had convinced me that I had done wrong, but because I was hurt by the first sharp word she had ever given me. . ..

... One day near the end of my second term at school the principal came into our room, and, after talking to the teacher, for some reason said: "I wish all of the white scholars to stand for a moment." I rose with the others. The teacher looked at me and, calling my name, said: "You sit down for the present, and rise with the others." I sat down dazed. I saw and heard nothing. When the others were asked to rise, I did not know it. When school was dismissed, I went out in a kind of stupor. A few of the white boys jeered at me, saying: "We knew he was coloured." "Shiny" said to them: "Come along, don't tease him," and thereby won my undying gratitude.'

[Source: *The Autobiography of an Ex-coloured Man* by James Weldon Johnson (Alfred A. Knopf Inc.). Reproduced in *Sociology Through Literature* edited by Lewis A. Coser (Prentice Hall)]

a) It has been suggested that at that time in the American South the social structure had some of the characteristics of a *caste system*. What is meant by that?

b) Why do you think the school principal asked the 'white scholars' to stand first?

c) Discuss some of the reasons why the white children might have been encouraged to look down on the coloured children.

d) It is suggested that coloured children in the USA were *socialised* into accepting an inferior position. To what extent is the process similar for working-class children in England today?

4

a) Do any of the figures in Table 20 (opposite) surprise you?

b) Which activities are most closely connected with social class?

c) To what extent do these figures support the view that there are many important social-class differences in the use of leisure time?

d) Comment on any other aspects of this table which you found interesting.

5

'All societies have to live by mastering their environment, but the way primitive societies do this is very different from our own. First of all, what is regarded as work is very different. In a primitive society most economic effort is devoted to the production of food. Apart from satisfying hunger, activities such as hunting, fishing or gathering crops are much more interesting and meaningful than most jobs in an office or a factory in an industralised society. Activities which are essential for primitive people are pleasurable recreations for us. This does not mean that hunting and fishing are always completely enjoyable for primitive people – much of it is hard routine and dangerous work, but there is no equivalent in the technology of a primitive society to the completely monotonous factory work where

Table 20
Leisure Activities: by Social Class 1973 (GB)

Percentage in each class participating in leisure activity groups

	Professional	Employers and Managers	Intermediate non-manual	Junior non-manual	Skilled manual	Semi-skilled manual and personal services	Unskilled	Full-time students	Total
Active outdoor sports and games	37	25	24	17	19	11	8	39	17
Active indoor sports and games	18	12	12	10	12	6	4	28	10
Watching sports and games	11	12	11	9	14	8	7	16	10
Open air outings	31	26	30	25	20	16	13	21	21
Visits to buildings, museums etc.,	19	13	17	11	6	5	3	15	9
Cultural outings	27	20	27	22	14	13	10	48	18
Amateur music and dramatics	7	4	8	4	2	2	1	13	3
Going out for a meal/drink/dancing/bingo	68	65	62	58	61	50	46	65	56
Gardening, DIY, needlework, hobbies	63	58	58	51	48	43	40	30	48
Social and voluntary activities, visiting and entertaining	79	73	81	76	60	62	58	72	67
Betting, gambling, games of skill, and other activities	34	30	30	27	31	24	21	26	27

[Source: *General Household Survey, 1973* (HMSO)]

individual workers never see or understand the whole production process.'

a) The author says that most economic effort in primitive societies is devoted to the production of food. Is this true in our society? Explain your answer.
b) Explain why the nature of work is different in a primitive society from that of an industrial society.
c) Give three examples of activities which most people in our society regard as leisure pastimes but which are work in a primitive society.
b) Give two more examples of differences between primitive societies and our own society which are not mentioned in the above passage.

Further Reading

Roberts, K. *Leisure*. Longman
Tunstall, J. *The Fishermen*. MacGibbon and Kee
Frankenberg, R. *Communities in Britain*. Penguin
Butterworth, E. and Weir, D. *Social Problems of Modern Britain*. Fontana. (Chapter 10, 'work')
Worsley, p. (ed.) *Problems of Modern Society*. Penguin. (A collection of articles. See especially Part 2, 'Industrialisation')

10
Population

The social science which is concerned with the scientific study of human populations, especially their size, structure, and development, is called 'demography'. Demographers study population statistics and try to measure as accurately as possible the past rises and occasional falls in populations; they also attempt to predict what is likely to happen in the future. It is very useful for governments to know exactly how many houses, school places, or hospital beds are likely to be needed at a given date (even if they often fail to take advantage of the predictions), so demographers are frequently employed by government departments to study the structure of populations past, present, and future, including the age structure of the population. It is very important to know, for example, what proportion of the population will be dependent, working, and retired in fifteen or twenty years' time. The statistical calculations used for prediction may be very complicated, but basically demographers calculate changes in population by observing the changes in just three factors: the *birth rate*, the *death rate*, and *migration* in and out of the country.

Sociologists rely heavily on demographic data when discussing population trends; but their concern is not simply to get the figures right, but to describe and explain the causes and the consequences of population changes.

1 Population Growth

Let us start with a known fact – the steady growth in population of the United Kingdom.

The evidence for the graph in Table 21 is very good. It is based on census figures collected every ten years since 1801 (except the wartime period 1941). The evidence for years before 1801 is less good – based on estimates rather than accurate figures – but it has been suggested, and generally accepted, that at the time of the Doomsday survey in the eleventh century the population of the whole of the area now

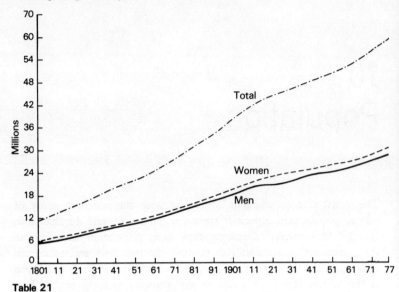

Table 21
Population Growth. Overall Size of Population: United Kingdom

[Source: *Britain in Figures* by A. F. Sillitoe (Penguin) and *Social Trends* no. 9, 1979 (HMSO)]

known as the United Kingdom was only about one and a half million. The following extract from the Registrar General's Statistical Review gives the actual figures from the ten-yearly Censuses:

1871	27 431 000
1881	31 014 000
1891	34 264 000
1901	38 236 000
1911	42 081 000
1921	44 027 000
1931	46 038 000
1951	50 225 000
1961	52 708 000
1971	55 200 000

The following figures give estimates of the population at the next four censuses:

1981	55 697 000
1991	56 712 000
2001	57 535 000
2011	57 706 000

[Source: *Facts in Focus*, 1978, Table 1 (HMSO.)]

Why has there been a continuous rise in the population of the United Kingdom?

130

2 Birth Rate

At the same time as the population has been rising, the actual birth rate and the number of children per family have fallen. It is necessary to understand the use of the term 'birth rate' as a precise technical term. The birth rate is a means of measuring accurately the frequency of births related to the entire population. In order to calculate the birth rate, three kinds of information are required:

1. the number of births in a given period of time – conventionally fixed at one year;
2. the number of people in the area for which the birth rate is being calculated – in this case the United Kingdom;
3. accurate information about when the births occurred.

Usually the birth rate is expressed as the number of births per 1000 persons in the population per year. Unless otherwise stated birth rate should always be understood as births per 1000 persons per year. The birth rate is therefore a measure of *fertility*; that is, the birth rate measures accurately the number of babies being born in a community compared with the number of people already existing in the community – it is not the same as *fecundity*, which is not nearly so easily measured and is concerned with the potentiality of producing children rather than the actual number of children born.

Table 22
Total Live Births per 1000 Population of All Ages

Date	Birth rate per annum
1871–1880	35·5
1881–1890	32·5
1891–1900	29·9
1901–1905	28·2
1906–1910	26·3
1911–1915	23·6
1916–1920	20·0
1921–1925	19·9
1926–1930	16·7
1931–1935	15·0
1936–1940	14·7
1941–1945	15·9
1946–1950	18·0
1951–1955	15·3
1956–1960	16·4
1961–1965	18·1
1966–1970	16·9
1974	16·2
1975	16·0
1976	15·5
1977	15·8

[Source: Census figures and *Social Trends* (HMSO)]

Table 22 gives us the crude demographic data. Sociologists then have to try to explain *why* the birth rate has fallen. To meet obvious suggestions first, it is perhaps necessary to state that there is no reason to believe that the frequency of sexual intercourse has delined: if anything it is probably higher than ever before: more people are now married, they get married earlier, and they are better fed and healthier – all of these factors would tend to increase rather than diminish sexual activity (and fecundity).

The second most obvious suggestion is that the birth rate has fallen because of the availability of contraceptive devices; but this is only partly true. It is sociologically naive to think that people will always limit the size of their family if it is possible to do so. The really important factor in family-size limitation is whether people *want* to limit the number of their children; good contraceptive techniques may certainly help them to succeed in their intentions, but it is the *intention* itself which is most important. For example, in many traditional, under-developed countries like India there is today a problem of too many people and too little food. Well-meaning Western agencies, such as the International Planned Parenthood Federation, have found that merely supplying contraceptives does little to solve the problem; the real difficulty is to change the *attitude* of the people towards size of family. On the other hand, there have been clear examples of countries which have reduced the population without artificial contraceptives: Ireland's birth rate dropped dramatically in the nineteenth century (after the potato famines), but the use of contraceptives was *not* a significant factor in this reduction.

The sociological question we have to ask about England at the end of the nineteenth century is, therefore, 'Why did people begin to want to have smaller families?' The answer is not entirely straight-forward, but has been sorted out in an excellent study by J. A. Banks, *Prosperity and Parenthood* (1954). This study showed that an important feature of the 1870's was that middle-class incomes remained steady but the cost of living rose – especially the expense of rearing children (nannies were for example considered essential). Education and getting older children settled in suitable employment were also extremely expensive. In other words, if they were to keep up their standard of living, middle-class parents had to find some way of economising, and the obvious means of doing this was to reduce the number of dependent children. The motivation to reduce the size of families was very strong, and middle-class parents began to make use of contraceptive devices such as the sheath or condom, which had in fact been available for many years before but had not become popular.

It is perfectly true that at about this time Charles Bradlaugh and Annie

Bessant were prosecuted for publishing a book about contraception called *The Fruits of Philosophy*, and the famous trial which took place in 1877 gave a great deal of publicity to the whole question of contraception. But it would be wrong to exaggerate the effect this had – it may have made the public more aware of the possibility of contraception but not of its desirability, which was the key factor.

The decline of the birth rate since that date is largely the story of the spread of the habit of family limitation down the social scale, at first to the lower-middle classes and by the twentieth century to working-class parents. In both cases the key factor was motivation of an economic kind – to reduce the number of dependent children in order to preserve or improve the standards of living. In the case of working-class families it has sometimes been suggested that an important cause was the 1870 Education Act, combined with the various Factory Acts forbidding child labour. The legislation which made education compulsory for

Table 23
Size of Family in Relation to Date of First Marriage, Great Britain, Marriages under 45 Years of Age, 1870–1925

| Live births per woman | Date of first marriage | | | |
| | 1870–9 | 1900–9 | 1915 | 1925 |
	Number of women per 1000 with specified number of live births			
0	83	113	150	161
1	53	148	212	252
2	72	187	235	254
3, 4	181	277	254	221
5, 6	189	147	94	72
7, 8, 9	245	99	45	34
10 or more	177	29 .	10	6

[Source: *A Survey of Social Conditions in England and Wales as illustrated by Statistics* by A. M. Carr-Saunders, D. Caradog Jones, and C. A. Moser © 1958 Oxford University Press (by permission of The Clarendon Press, Oxford)]

Table 24
Fertility According to Social Class, GB

| Social Class | Number of children | |
	1951[1]	1971[2]
1. Professional etc. occupations	1·88	2·26
2. Intermediate occupations	2·00	2·18
3N. Skilled non-manual occupations	2·36	2·02
3M. Skilled manual occupations		2·37
4. Partly-skilled occupations	2·78	2·40
5. Unskilled occupations	3·18	2·74
All	2·44	2·33

(1 Average no. of legitimate live-born children to women aged 20–24 at marriage, married only once, whose marriages had lasted for 20–24 years.
2 Average no. of live-born children to women in first marriage at 1971 census, whose marriages had lasted for 15–19 years.)
[Source: A Survey of *Social Conditions in England and Wales as illustrated by statistics* by A. M. Carr-Saunders, D. Caradog-Jones and C. A. Moser, © 1958 Oxford University Press (by permission of The Clarendon Press, Oxford), and *Demographic Review 1977* (HMSO)]

Table 25
Population changes and projections

United Kingdom

	Census enumerated				Mid-year estimates			Projections[2]			
	1901–11	1911–21	1921–31	1931–51	1951–61	1961–71	1971–72	1972–81	1981–91	1991–2001	2001–11
De facto population at start of period (millions)	38·2	42·1	44·0	46·0	50·3	52·8	55·6	55·9	57·3	59·8	62·4
Average annual change (thousands)											
Live births	1091	975	824	785	839	962	865	873	993	1000	1034
Deaths	624	689[1]	555	598[1]	593	638	661	669	692	686	668
Net natural change	467	286	268	188	246	324	204	204	300	313	366
Net civilian migration	−82	−92	−67	+22	−7	−32	−30	−50	−50	−50	−50
Net changes from deployment of armed forces between UK and elsewhere					+13	−12[3]	+14				
Overall annual change	385	195	201	213	252	280	188[4]	154	250	263	316

1 Including deaths of non-civilians and merchant seamen who died outside the country.
2 Projections based on the provisional mid-1972 estimate of *total* population, which has subsequently been revised.
3 The England and Wales component includes changes in armed forces, in visitor balance and balancing adjustments to reconcile population increase between 1961 and 1971 Censuses with estimates of natural increase and net civilian migration.
4 The mid-1972 estimates for Northern Ireland is based on a population figure for 1971, revised in the light of the 1971 Census results, of 1538·0 thousand.

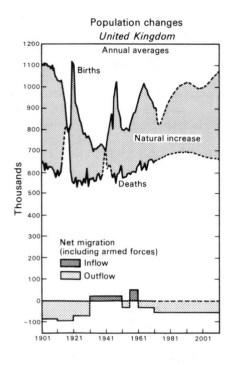

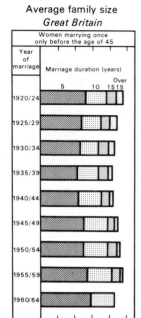

[Source: *Social Trends* no. 4 (HMSO)]

working-class children had the effect of making children an economic liability, rather than an asset – they cost money to feed and clothe, rather than being wage earners contributing to the family income. The evidence on this specific point is lacking, but eventually, the general economic reasons for reducing the number of children certainly applied to working-class as well as to middle-class parents, although even today there are differences in family size corresponding to social-class groupings.

The persistence of this social-class difference is also of sociological (and demographic) interest. Why should working-class parents produce more children? To some extent it might be that they use less efficient methods of birth control, such as coitus interruptus (withdrawal), but this is unlikely to be the complete explanation. The conventional sociological explanation is that some working-class families – especially the traditional working-class families – *want* more children because they are less concerned with social mobility of their children and more concerned with a rich and flourishing family life.

135

3 The Decline in the Death Rate

Returning to the general question of size of population in our society, we must explain the rising population in the UK not in terms of a rising birth rate but a lower death rate. This fall in the death rate is much easier to explain. The death rate is calculated in a very similar way to the birth rate, described above. To calculate the official death rate we need to know the number of deaths in a given year and the number of people in the area for which the death rate is being calculated, i.e. England and Wales or the United Kingdom. The death rate is then expressed as so many deaths per 1000 persons per year.

Table 26
Expectation of Life

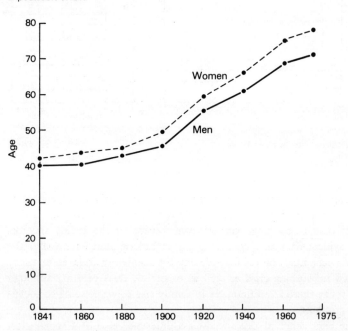

Thus, where we have a falling death rate without an equivalent fall in the birth rate, the population will rise unless there is a loss of population by emigration. Since 1870 we have had a falling birth rate but *an even greater fall in the death rate* (the less important effect of migration will be considered later in the chapter).

Another way of looking at this particular aspect of a falling death rate is to examine the expectation of life. *Expectation of life* can be

Table 27
Death Rate per 1000 Population of All Ages

Date	Death rate per annum
1861–1870	22·5
1871–1880	21·4
1881–1890	19·1
1891–1900	18·2
1901–1910	15·4
1911–1920	14·4
1921–1930	12·1
1931–1940	12·3
1941–1950	12·4
1951–1960	11·8
1961–1970	11·7

More recent figures tend to give death rates by sex because of the wide variation between the sexes:

	Males	Females
1974	15·3	9·2
1975	15·1	9·0
1976	15·3	9·2

[Source: Census figures and *Social Trends* (HMSO)]

estimated from any age. The Registrar General gives Tables for expectation of life at birth and also at the age of fifteen, forty-five, and sixty-five years. For many purposes it is sufficient simply to look at the expectation a person has of living from the time of birth expressed as an average for the total number of babies born at a given time.

Sociologists are interested in finding out what they can about *why* people are living longer now than they did a hundred years ago. The causes in the fall of the death rate and the greater expectation of life are fairly well established: the better standards in health and medical services in the nineteenth century, and more recently the extension of welfare services. Killer diseases such as cholera have virtually disappeared, mainly as a result of improved sanitation and public health, but partly due to better medical services and, since the last war, the National Health Service. Other aspects of the Welfare State, such as housing and the elimination of gross poverty, have also contributed to a healthier and therefore longer-living society.

The effects of greater life expectation are also very important. Changes in life-expectation not only increase the size of a population; they also alter its age distribution. The age pyramids in Table 28 illustrate clearly the kind of changes which have taken place.

Of particular concern to planners are the proportions of children, workers, and retired people, since if there are too few workers carrying the burden of the other two 'dependent' groups then this may make increases in taxation inevitable. But other results of change are also important; for example, new towns which were planned for young couples and their children are often unsuitable when the young children grow into teenagers for whom there are few recreational facilities.

Table 28
Population

[Source: *Britain in Figures* by A. F. Sillitoe (Penguin)]

Age	1871 census Women	1871 census Men	1966 census Women	1966 census Men	2000 forecast Women	2000 forecast Men
Over 80	70000	100000	340000	780000	490000	1190000
75–79	100000	120000	440000	820000	660000	1100000
70–74	190000	220000	700000	1130000	910000	1230000
65–69	280000	290000	1040000	1400000	1170000	1320000
60–64	360000	410000	1430000	1650000	1390000	1450000
55–59	410000	450000	1660000	1800000	1620000	1640000
50–54	550000	600000	1720000	1820000	2040000	2020000
45–49	600000	650000	1700000	1740000	1900000	1850000
40–44	700000	770000	1820000	1810000	2070000	1990000
35–39	760000	840000	1730000	1680000	2380000	2300000
30–34	890000	980000	1700000	1610000	2380000	2310000
25–29	1000000	1130000	1740000	1680000	2670000	2490000
20–24	1140000	1270000	1940000	1870000	2720000	2620000
15–19	1320000	1340000	2200000	2100000	2850000	2710000
10–14	1490000	1460000	1940000	1850000	3040000	2880000
5–9	1630000	1630000	2170000	2060000	3250000	3080000
Under 5	1850000	1840000	2470000	2340000	3440000	3260000

I have already mentioned in Chapter 9 one problem of an ageing population, namely that elderly retired people have less money but more time and a narrower range of interests. This may well be a growing problem for the United Kingdom.

The geographical structure of the population is also important. There are regional differences in the United Kingdom for educational opportunity, employment, and housing. The people in the north tend to be less privileged in many ways, and there is a tendency for the population to drift to the more prosperous areas, especially in the south-east.

Immigration and Emigration

Most of the statistics quoted so far in this chapter show the fall in the death rate or the rising expectation of life to be the most important factor in population growth over the country as a whole. We have not yet considered the effect of migration on population in this country. Once again the relevant figures, of a highly reliable kind (but probably not 100% accurate), are obtainable from the Registrar General. If we are talking about the total population growth for the United Kingdom, the figure that we are interested in is net migration, that is, the balance between migration into the country and migration of British people out of the country to Europe or the Commonwealth or other parts of the world. The Table below gives the pattern from 1871 to the middle 1970's. Where the balance of migration is that emigrants exceed immigrants the figure is preceded by a minus sign, but where there are more immigrants than emigrants the figure is shown with a plus.

Table 29
Migration Net Gains and Losses, United Kingdom, 1871–1976

1871–1881	− 415 000
1881–1891	− 960 000
1891–1901	− 190 000
1901–1911	− 820 000
1911–1921	− 919 000
1921–1931	− 672 000
1931–1951	+ 465 000
1951–1961	+ 12 000
1961–1966	+ 74 000
1966–1967	− 88 000
1967–1968	− 37 000
1968–1969	− 54 000
1969–1970	− 60 000
1970–1971	− 39 000
1971–1972	− 44 000
1972–1973	− 5 000
1973–1974	− 77 000
1974–1975	− 72 000
1975–1976	− 29 000

The general picture over the last hundred years is that more people have emigrated than immigrated. Large numbers of immigrants entered the country in the 1930's just before the Second World War, when Jewish refugees and others escaped from Germany and other parts of Europe. Since the last war, the migration has generally been from the Commonwealth, especially India, Pakistan and the West Indies. It is still, however, true to say that more people have left the country than have entered.

In discussions about immigration, two extreme points of view can be heard. One extremist view tends to blame immigrants for all our social problems: housing, unemployment, crime, and diseases such as tuberculosis and VD. At the other extreme the opinion is sometimes put forward that immigrants are no different from native British people and therefore unrestricted numbers of immigrants could be allowed into the country without making any appreciable difference, or even that this unrestricted immigration would be desirable. Neither of these two points of view stands up to sociological analysis. Although immigration has increased, the immigrants from India, Pakistan, and the West Indies – the so-called 'coloured' immigrants and their immediate descendents – constitute less than 2% of our total population. We had a housing problem and unemployment long before coloured immifrants arrived in this country, and there is no evidence that immigrants in general are more responsible for crime and disease than any other section of the community.

But the other extreme point of view is equally fallacious. To suppose that large numbers of people from very different cultures from our own could come to this country and be absorbed or integrated without very careful preparation, planning, and a willingness to integrate is absurd. It is highly likely that, where people from different cultures have to live side by side, some friction will develop. It is also true that, although immigrants constitute only a very small percentage of the total population, they are concentrated into a few areas in the United Kingdom: various districts in London, Birmingham, Bradford, etc. It is not correct to use the word 'ghetto' for groupings of immigrants living in the urban centres, but it is certainly true that there are now areas which are largely occupied by people who were not born in this country or whose parents were not. One problem is that any group of people from a different culture settling in this country will find it more difficult for their children to adjust to our educational system and be 'successful' within it. Thus there is a considerable danger that West Indian children, for example, will be less successful in their education and in their career prospects than native-born white children, and that they will tend to be offered low-paid unattractive jobs or to join the ranks of the unemployed. If this were to happen there would be the danger of the kind of racial antagonism which already exists in parts of the USA. To avoid this kind of development, it is most important that adequate educational services are provided so that groups of second-class citizens do not emerge. This is particularly difficult when some groups of immigrants have a first language other than English, or speak a 'non-standard' variety of English.

Population Growth

It is clear, therefore, that population growth has been mainly caused by better medical and health services which have brought about a decline in the death rate. There would have been an even greater increase in population if the birth rate had not also declined at the same time. The effect of migration on population growth is very small indeed.

Table 30
People born overseas

Great Britain

	1931	1951	1961	1966	1971[2]
Birthplace					
Number of people (thousands)[1]:					
Foreign countries[3]	347	722	842	886	980
Canada, Australia, New Zealand	75	99	110	125	143
Other Commonwealth	137	218	541	853	1151
Irish Republic[4]	362	532	709	732	709
Total born overseas	921	1571	2202	2596	2983
As percentage of population:					
Foreign countries[3]	0·8	1·5	1·6	1·7	1·8
Canada, Australia, New Zealand	0·2	0·2	0·2	0·2	0·3
Other Commonwealth	0·3	0·4	1·1	1·6	2·1
Irish Republic[4]	0·8	1·1	1·4	1·4	1·3
Total born overseas	2·0	3·2	4·3	5·0	5·5

[1] Persons resident in Great Britain at the time of the Census who had been born outside the United Kingdom; including United Kingdom citizens born overseas but excluding short-term visitors.
[2] Final 1971 Census figures.
[3] Including South Africa.
[4] Including Ireland (part not stated).

Problems of a Growing Population

A growing population is not necessarily a problem – the comparative affluence of industrialised Britain would not have been possible without the growth in numbers in the eighteenth and nineteenth centuries – but few would deny that there must be a maximum number of people who can be fed adequately and live in the world without overcrowding. The same applies to individual countries, including the United Kingdom. When people talk of 'the problem of over-population' they are often referring to India or developing countries, but in many respects the problem in developed countries such as the United Kingdom is even greater – so much so that some are calling for 'zero population growth', i.e. no further rise in numbers at all.

The population *density* of the United Kingdom (i.e. the number of people per square mile) is one of the highest in the world: we have about 225 people to the square kilometre compared with about 75 per square kilometre in China. We have to import about half of all the food we need, and even if we were immediately to succeed in

Table 31
Population in the regions

| | United Kingdom | | | | Mid-year estimates | | | | Percentages Projections[3] | |
| | Census | | | | | | | | | |
Standard regions of England[1]:	1901	1911	1921	1931	1951	1961	1971[2]	1972[2]	1981	1991
North	6·5	6·7	6·9	6·6	6·2	6·1	5·9	5·9	5·8	5·7
Yorkshire and Humberside	9·2	9·3	9·3	9·4	9·0	8·8	8·7	8·6	8·5	8·4
East Midlands	5·3	5·3	5·3	5·5	5·8	5·9	6·1	6·1	6·4	6·6
East Anglia	3·0	2·8	2·8	2·7	2·8	2·8	3·0	3·1	3·3	3·4
South East	27·5	27·8	27·9	29·4	30·2	31·0	31·0	31·0	30·9	30·9
South West	6·7	6·4	6·2	6·1	6·5	6·5	6·8	6·9	7·0	7·1
West Midlands	7·8	7·8	8·0	8·1	8·8	9·0	9·2	9·2	9·3	9·2
North West	13·8	13·8	13·6	13·4	12·8	12·4	12·1	12·1	12·0	11·9
Wales	5·3	5·8	6·0	5·6	5·1	5·0	4·9	4·9	4·8	4·8
Scotland	11·7	11·3	11·1	10·5	10·1	9·8	9·4	9·3	9·2	9·1
Northern Ireland	3·2	3·0	2·9	2·7	2·7	2·7	2·8	2·8	2·8	2·9
Total de facto population —%	100·0	100·0	100·0	100·0	100·0	100·0	100·0	100·0	100·0	100·0
—millions	38·2	42·1	44·0	46·0	50·3	52·8	55·6	55·8	57·7	60·2

1 Boundaries as at 1971.
2 Figures relate to the revised estimates of population based on the final results of the 1971 Census.
3 Projections of home population based on the provisional mid-1971 estimate, which has subsequently been revised.

Table 32
Migrant flows by region, 1971

Thousands

	Into United Kingdom			Out from United Kingdom			Balance		
	Males	Females	Total	Males	Females	Total	Males	Females	Total
Standard regions of England:									
North	2·2	2·7	4·9	5·6	2·9	8·5	−3·4	−0·2	−3·6
Yorkshire and Humberside	6·0	4·7	10·7	8·7	6·5	15·2	−2·7	−1·8	−4·5
East Midlands	4·4	2·9	7·3	5·6	5·5	11·2	−1·3	−2·6	−3·9
East Anglia	2·1	2·0	4·1	2·8	2·9	5·7	−0·7	−0·9	−1·6
South East	60·5	55·2	115·7	53·8	59·6	113·4	+6·7	−4·4	+2·3
South West	4·6	5·2	9·7	5·9	5·8	11·7	−1·3	−0·6	−1·9
West Midlands	6·8	5·9	12·7	9·0	6·3	15·3	−2·2	−0·4	−2·6
North West	8·2	8·9	17·1	15·2	12·3	27·5	−7·0	−3·4	−10·4
Wales	2·2	2·3	4·6	2·7	2·5	5·3	−0·5	−0·2	−0·7
Scotland	5·0	5·9	10·9	12·6	9·7	22·3	−7·6	−3·8	−11·4
Northern Ireland	0·4	1·1	1·5	2·1	1·6	3·7	−1·7	−0·5	−2·2
UK not stated	0·2	0·2	0·4	0·1	0·2	0·3	+0·1	—	+0·1
All migrants into and out from the United Kingdom	102·7	97·0	199·7	124·2	115·8	240·0	−21·5	−18·8	−40·4

Note: Based on the self-description of a migrant in the International Passenger survey.
[Source: *Social Trends* no. 4, 1973 (HMSO)]

avoiding any further increase in population we would still lose rather than gain farmland – every year agricultural land is sacrificed for new roads or housing developments.

Apart from the problem of food supplies, we have to ask questions about the *quality of life* in over-populated regions. Some would suggest that the quality of life is not a proper concern of sociologists, but I would not share this view. I mentioned in earlier chapters the increasing demand for leisure, which is often frustrated by lack of facilities – the larger the population, the more difficult it is to solve other social problems such as unemployment, housing, and creating tolerable urban environments.

The last question will be referred to again in the next chapter.

Questions for Discussion and/or Written Work

I

The Projected Increase in the Population of the United Kingdom, 1969–2001

Increase due to	Percentage change	Change in millions
a declining mortality rates	+2½	+1½
b excess of births over deaths	+17	+9½
c effects of immigration and emigration	nil	nil
Overall increase	+20	+11

[Source: Adapted from *Social Trends* no. 3, 1972 (HMSO)]

i) What is the most important cause of the increase in population projected?
ii) Explain clearly what is meant by the three kinds of increase: (a), (b), and (c).
iii) What are the most important consequences that may result from an increase in population in the United Kingdom?

2

Table 33
Average Life Expectation at Birth, England and Wales
[Source: *Britain in Figures* by A. F. Sillitoe (Penguin)]

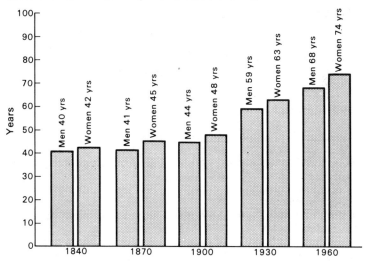

a) Explain carefully what is meant by *expectation of life*.
b) In general, who tend to live longer – men or women? Try to explain why this might be so.
c) Give as many reasons as possible to explain why both men and women tend to live longer now than a hundred years ago.
d) What is meant by *infant-mortality rate*? Explain the connection between infant-mortality rate and average life expectation.
e) How would you expect a table showing the average life expectation for *one* of the developing countries to differ from the table shown above?

3

The Conservation Society

The Conservation Society was founded to make people more aware of the effects on our environment of the population explosion and the unwise use of technology, and to do something about it.

Many bodies concern themselves with different aspects of conservation, such as preserving the countryside, wildlife, and historic buildings. We sympathise with all of these, and with ad hoc campaigns against specific and immediate threats to the environment. But we believe that piecemeal measures are not enough.

The fundamental threat lies in nonstop growth of population and material demands on the environment. Unless these are tackled, conservation measures can only be short-term palliatives.

We want to educate ourselves, the public, technologists and the government to face the really basic question: growth of population and material consumption versus resources within the whole balance of nature.

The Basic Facts

The World: In the last 170 years numbers have doubled twice, to 3900 million. The rate of growth is accelerating, and at present rates population will double every 37 years. We shall have a staggering 7000 million shortly after the turn of the century. Already over half of the world's people are malnourished. Even if food production manages to keep up with population, this proportion will simply come to represent millions more hungry human beings.

There are 200 000 more people in the world today than there were yesterday. Think what that means not just in terms of food for their lifetime, but in education, transport, housing, recreation, and all the other facilities and services necessary to life. For many of them there is little enough chance of a healthy life – almost none at all of a happy one.

At the same time, industry is growing faster than ever before, in order to support larger populations and greater demand from them for material goods. The raw materials upon which our civilisation depends, which have taken millions of years to accumulate, are now being used so rapidly that we will very soon face severe shortages.

We can no longer say that we are approaching the limits of the earth's ability to absorb our pressures upon it and regenerate fresh resources; we have already overstepped them, perhaps permanently. Consider our three most basic needs: air, water, and soil. Emission of poisonous gases creates murderous smogs over many of the world's major cities. Many of the world's large lakes are dying, and the oceans themselves are seriously threatened. Rash farming methods have turned thousands of square miles of once rich land to desert, and lowered the quality of far more.

The United Kingdom: Our population started its rapid expansion 200 years ago. Since then, it has increased sevenfold, to 56 million and is expected to increase by a further 6 million by the end of the century. To house them means building equivalent to 15 cities the size of Nottingham, or one greater London. Already an area the size of Worcestershire disappears under concrete and asphalt every decade.

Our population density is among the highest in the world. The United Kingdom has 595 people to the square mile: three times as many as China, eleven times as many as the U.S.A. Half our food is imported. As agricultural land shrinks while population soars this proportion must increase, with further dependence on the uncertain food surpluses of other countries.

The Effect on you

Noise, dirt, smell: only at very great cost – unlikely to be forthcoming – shall we be able to delay the spread of all kinds of environmental pollution.

Loss of heritage: old towns, picturesque villages, historic buildings, and beautiful countryside are disappearing at an evergrowing rate.

Wildlife in danger: over forty species of animals have become extinct in the last fifty years. More will follow unless we change our ways.

Room to breathe: human beings need open space for health and happiness; there will soon be far less of it, but demand for outdoor recreation is expected to triple in the next decade.

Daily activities: many routine chores, like shopping and travelling to work, will continue to grow more exasperating and time-consuming.

Mental health: there is growing evidence that the crowding of cities – with shrinking opportunities for necessary peace and solitude – is taking its toll on mental health. And each year the cities sprawl further.

Individual dignity: governing large, tightly packed numbers efficiently must lead to policies which treat people more and more as ciphers than as individuals. Eventually, constraints on personal freedom – such as when and where you may go on holiday – will be necessary.

What we must do

We accept President Kennedy's definition of conservation as ' . . . the wise use of our natural environment, prevention of waste, pre-serving, improving, and renewing all our resources.' We stress the improvement and wise use of our resources in addition to the pre-servation of our heritage for those who come after us.

We advocate an ecological approach to human problems under-standing and working with, rather than against, the basic relations between living things and their environment. We must make life in an environment of high quality our chief goal, and start working for it now. If we fail, we deprive posterity of most of its freedom of choice and of the basic rights and amenities we enjoy. Dust bowls, polluted rivers, and sprawling suburbs are easy to create but hard to abolish.

Desperate attempts to provide ever-increasing populations with food, and ever-expanding economies with raw materials and dumping grounds for waste, make the misuse of science and technology almost inevitable. The stabilisation of population and the conversion of the economy from reckless exploitation to the cyclical system of the space-ship are problems that must be tackled simultaneously.

Man cannot indefinitely modify either his society or the earth itself; even if he could, it would not be possible to maintain the quality of life. Nor can he continue to squander the earth's limited resources without regard to our needs beyond the next few years. The choice is

between a policy which regulates our numbers and economic behaviour, and catastrophe.'

[Source: Leaflet *The Conservation Society*, with amendments by
the society]

a) What are the main reasons for concern about increasing world
   population?
b) What are the particular problems of population growth in the
   United Kingdom?
c) Why have many attempts to reduce the rate of population growth
   failed?
d) What help might sociologists give in solving population problems?

Table 34
Migration into and out from the United Kingdom, by nationality and country of
last permanent or intended future residence

	Thousands	
	1976	
	In	Out
Total migrants	179·8	210·4
Commonwealth citizens	129·9	165·5
Country of last permanent or intended future residence:		
Commonwealth countries		
Total	87·6	89·9
Australia	24·4	31·5
Canada	7·3	22·0
New Zealand	8·1	9·0
African countries	17·7	10·7
India, Bangladesh and Sri Lanka	9·2	3·6
West Indies	3·6	3·4
Other countries	17·4	9·8
Foreign countries		
Total	42·4	75·6
South Africa	7·9	19·6
Latin America	6·4	10·6
United States	1·7	1·8
Western Europe	17·4	22·7
Other countries	8·9	20·8
Aliens	49·8	44·9
Country of last permanent or intended future residence:		
Commonwealth countries	0·9	1·2
Foreign countries		
Total	48·9	43·6
United States	10·0	10·3
EEC countries	9·8	13·6
Other Western European countries and Eastern Europe	9·0	7·7
Other countries	20·1	12·0

[Source: *Facts in Focus*, 1978, compiled by the Central Statistical Office (HMSO)]

a) In 1976 did migration increase or decrease the population in the
   United Kingdom? By how many?

b) Where did most migrants in 1976 come from?
c) Why have governments in recent years restricted immigration?
d) Discuss some of the problems faced by immigrants in the UK.

5
a) Why are sociologists interested in population?
b) What is the difference between demography and sociology?

Further Reading

Kelsall, R. K. *Population*. Longman
Butterworth, E. and Weir, D. *Social Problems of Modern Britain*. Fontana. (Chapters 4 and 5)
Kent, G. *Poverty*. Batsford (Past into Present Series)
Worsley, P. (ed.) *Problems of Modern Society*. Penguin. (Part 1, 'Population, Resources and Pollution')

11
Social Stability and Change

People often think of sociologists in connection with social problems, and it is common for sociologists to be confused with social workers. Many social workers have studied some sociology, but not all sociologists are social workers. It is true that sociologists tend to be interested in social problems, but they do study other aspects of society. Sociologists are interested in the 'normal' functioning of society, but their names are more likely to get into the headlines and catch the attention of the public when they make statements about violence or delinquency or illegitimacy.

Most sociologists are certainly just as interested in normality as in abnormality, or social pathology, and they are just as interested in social stability as in change. On the other hand I did suggest in Chapter 1 that the origins of sociology were associated with rapid social change – especially the industrial and political revolutions of the eighteenth and nineteenth centuries. Sociologists were concerned to *explain* change; others, like Durkheim, were frankly worried about the rapidity of change and looked for methods of ensuring that society did not break down completely.

Urbanisation

One of the most important changes in our history was the transformation of English society from a rural, agricultural economy to an urban, industrial economy. The feudal system, where power was closely connected with *land* ownership, gradually gave way to a *capitalist* economy in which power was in the hands of the owners of the means of producing goods (not just food), that is, factory owners and financiers – the 'capitalists' or 'bourgeoisie', as Marx referred to them. Our eighteenth- and nineteenth-century political history was very much concerned with the struggle between the Tory Party, which largely represented the land-owning aristocracy and *landed* gentry, and the new

Whig Party, which largely represented the rich manufacturers – the owners of *capital*, or the bourgeoisie. An important part of this change and of the Industrial Revolution itself was the growth of towns, or the process of urbanisation.

Sociologists are interested in urbanisation for a number of reasons. Living in towns is very different from living in the country in several important aspects. In a country village everyone tends to know every-one else, and the community is close-knit. The relation of the family to the rest of the community structure is clear; rules and norms of be-haviour tend to be well established and clear-cut. 'Community' implies having something in common. It is easy to see the kind of things that people in rural communities had in common (and still have); it is much more difficult to see what makes up a community in towns or cities. When people had to leave their rural communities during the Industrial Revolution and seek out work and homes in towns and cities, they faced very important changes. Perhaps the most striking change would be the comparative anonymity of living in a town: people would certainly not know everyone else; they might have some kind of community with their near neighbours, but beyond that limited territory they were unknown strangers. This probably has some connection with the much higher crime and delinquency rates in towns – it is much more a temptation to steal from strangers than from neighbours: rules which apply to people you know well are not always automatically transferred to 'outsiders'. This is one of the difficulties of towns – establishing a workable basis of law and order.

It is also true that work in towns, as we saw in earlier chapters, tends to be impersonal and less meaningful. Even if people had been exploited as farm labourers, they were at least aware of the usefulness of their work in the fields: it had a definite meaning for them. This was not so with work in the urban factories, so one important meaningful aspect of life was removed.

Many sociologists have written about the differences between industrial urban society and pre-industrial rural communities. Some sociologists make a distinction between *folk* society and *urban* society. The folk society or community will be small, isolated, and possess a strong sense of group solidarity. Behaviour tends to be of a traditional kind, which means that it will be spontaneous in the sense of not involving many conscious decisions. It will also tend to be uncritical and personal. There is little choice compared with living in urban society. People tend to get on with things without thinking about them. The family and kinship are very important units in the community. On the other hand, urban societies have been characterised as being much less homogeneous, that is, people tend to be different from each other in many ways. This tends to make urban communities appear to be less organised; the family and kinship is often less important; there is a tendency for the market economy to be the dominant value system; religion is also less likely to be important than in folk society.

The words often associated with urbanisation are such features of modern industrial town life as poverty, crime, and delinquency. This is not to say that there was no poverty or crime in the pre-industrial village – if you have studied any social history you will know that that is quite untrue – but there does appear to be a strong tendency in urbanised societies for poverty and delinquency to exist side by side with affluence in such a way as to suggest that if only urban life were better organised such problems could be made to disappear. It is the complexity, size, and difficulty of organisation in urban life which appears to cause problems.

The British city of 1 million would contain:

>5 000 mentally handicapped,
>160 000 old-age pensioners,
>30 000 criminals or delinqients,
>35 000 people without jobs,
>150 000 lonely or depressed,
>300 000 inadequately housed.

(From a speech by Peter Walker when he was Minister of the Environment)

Poverty

Poverty is by no means entirely an urban problem. If we think of poverty as a world-wide problem, the most poverty-striken areas are certainly the non-industrialised, under-developed rural countries such as India. It is also true that in our own history poverty was a feature of Elizabethan England, for example – hence the Elizabethan Poor Law. But poverty in England reached its peak as a problem after the Industrial Revolution when thousands of people crowded into towns with inadequate housing and food and frequent unemployment. I have already mentioned the pioneering work of Seebohm Rowntree who investigated poverty in York right at the end of the nineteenth century (1899) and also in later surveys. Up to this time, governments had always been reluctant to take on responsibility for the poor; the theory was that the poor should be helped by their own family or, if that failed, by the parish – that is, the local community. This local 'parish' system was never completely effective, even in rural England, but with the coming of industrialisation the system broke down completely. But still governments refused to see poverty as a national problem – the poor were condemned as idlers and scroungers. One of Rowntree's contributions was to demonstrate that this was not true: he showed that many hard-working and careful families simply could not make ends meet. Another of his contributions was to calculate a poverty line (that is, the income for any particular family below which it was impossible to maintain life in a healthy way). He also investigated the *causes* of poverty. He found that in a quarter of the families living below the poverty line in York the chief wage-earner was dead, disabled, ill, or unemployed. But in about half of the cases the father of the family was in work but did not earn enough to support the family adequately.

Over seventy years later, this is still a major reason for poverty in our society. Although the provisions of the Welfare State now make it

x

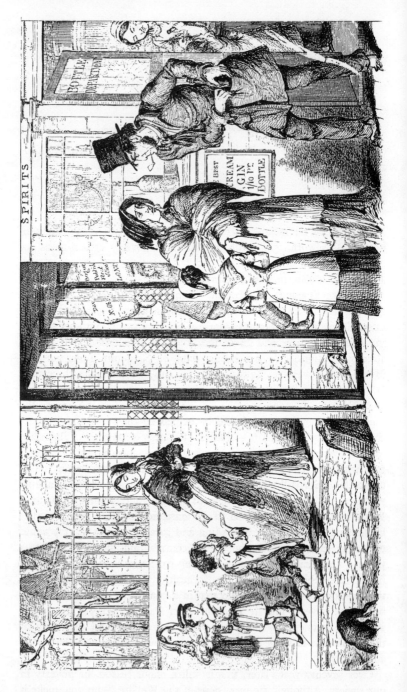

unnecessary for people to starve, they may continue to experience hardship. The National Health and Social Security Service does now ensure minimum standards of well-being, and supplements can be made to families whose income is below a poverty line (now defined at a rather higher level than in 1899), but the problem of poverty has by no means been solved. Housing difficulties still exist in towns, unemployment and sickness still cause considerable hardship, and a few people die of starvation every year. The Welfare State has recognised that it is the problem of society as a whole to look after needy members, but it has not yet solved the problem of reaching all those members of society who are in need of help. It is also true that, despite some measure of equalisation of incomes, there is still a very wide gap indeed between the poorest members of society and the richest. Successive governments have failed to provide a means of redistributing income in such a way as to abolish poverty completely.

There has been an important change in attitudes to poverty since the early nineteenth century. The Welfare State developed largely as a result of this change, and should be seen as an increasing awareness of national responsibility and developing consciousness of social justice or fairness, rather than as a simple series of government Acts. There are many good introductory books on the Welfare State which set out these changes very clearly (see the list of further reading at the end of this chapter).

Crime and Delinquency

Another aspect of modern, industrial societies which is often discussed is the high rate of crime and delinquency. Most societies have problems of delinquency, but it is certainly true that they are more common in urban societies. It is, of course, also true that different societies do not entirely agree about what constitutes crime: bigamy is a crime in England but not in Muslim countries; drinking alcohol is forbidden in some societies but tolerated in others. On the other hand there is general agreement that murder, rape, and robbery should be forbidden by law. And changes in the law do occur – fairly recently in England, for example, certain forms of abortion and homosexual behaviour have ceased to be illegal. Customs change, ideas about morality change to some extent, and laws change. There is also no total equivalence of law and morality in our society – not everything which is regarded as immoral is illegal – but there is some agreement. One view of the difference between delinquency and crime is based on the question of morality and legality: serious offences against custom or moral codes may be termed as delinquent, but only actually breaking the law is a crime. There is of course some degree of correspondence, and most *serious* offences against morality do tend to be acts of crime, but there are certain areas of behaviour which are generally thought to be immoral which are not crimes, and occasionally there are laws which people do not generally consider to be connected with morality (for example, few people breaking the thirty-miles-per-hour speed limit would think of themselves as immoral, although they know they are breaking the law). One of the problems of complex industrial societies is to persuade people that what is regarded as illegal should also be accepted as morally undesirable.

It is probably true that the number of people breaking laws changes from time to time, but actually measuring such changes is not as easy as it seems. Table 35 shows a rise in 'offences recorded by the police' from 638,000 in 1951 to 2,810,000 in 1977. This is clear enough, but there are difficulties in *interpreting* such figures, and, although it is true that this probably reflects a rise in 'criminality', it does not necessarily mean that the increase of nearly four and a half times suggested by the Table is correct.

Table 35
Offences recorded by the police: persons proceeded against, and persons found guilty (UK)

	Thousands							
	1951	1961	1966	1971	1974	1975	1976	1977
England and Wales								
Indictable offences recorded	547	868	1307	1666	1963	2106	2136	2463
Scotland								
Crimes	83	109	148	181	192	232	265	301
Northern Ireland								
Indictable offences	8	10	15	31	33	37	40	46
	638	987	1470	1878	2188	2375	2441	2810

[Source: *Social Trends* no. 9, 1979 (HMSO)]

Some crimes are never reported to the police and therefore do not get recorded as 'offences known to the police'. For example, some businessmen might hide sums of money at home because they have not declared it for income tax; if their house were burgled and the money stolen they would not necessarily feel inclined to report the theft to the police! In the past it may have been more common for policemen to deal with less serious offences informally rather than make out a long report – they might administer a stern reprimand to a young offender, or a 'clip round the ear'. It might also be true that a rise in offences known to the police *might* reflect the fact that fewer police are being bribed to conceal crimes. On the other hand, more efficient police work may actually produce a rise in such crime figures – i.e. offences known to the police are to a certain extent a reflection of police

Table 36
Crime: types of offence, England and Wales

Thousands

	1951	1961	1966	1971	1974	1975	1976	1977
Serious offences								
Burglary	—	—	—	452	484	522	515	604
Robbery	—	—	—	7	9	11	12	14
Theft and handling stolen goods	—	—	—	1004	1190	1268	1286	1488
Fraud and forgery	—	—	—	100	117	123	120	121
Total burglary, robbery, etc.	514	820	1247	1563	1800	1924	1933	2226
Violence against the person	7	18	27	47	64	71	78	82
Sexual offences	15	20	21	24	25	24	22	21
Criminal damage	5	6	10	27	67	79	93	124
Other offences	6	4	2	6	8	8	10	10
Total serious offences	547	868	1307	1666	1963	2106	2136	2463
Serious offences cleared up (percentages)	47	44	39	45	44	44	43	41
Persons found guilty:								
Serious offences	133	182	233	322	375	402	415	429
Other offences								
Assault	12	12	11	12	12	12	12	13
Drunkenness (non-motoring)	51	72	67	83	98	100	103	103
Drunken driving	{291	6	7	37	52	54	46	41
Other motoring offences		649	891	951	1121	1127	1179	1089
Malicious damage	9	15	17	20	—	—	—	—
Motor vehicle licences	6	21	40	85	85	94	102	86
Wireless and Telegraphy Acts	3	10	21	27	34	33	35	45
Other offences	213	187	159	152	157	167	179	173
Total other offences	584	970	1213	1366	1559	1587	1656	1550

[Source: *Social Trends* no. 9, 1979 (HMSO)]

vigilance. But, despite all this uncertainty about what they actually mean, crime statistics are useful, so long as we are not too willing to believe them in exactly the form in which they are presented. In other words, crime statistics, like all statistics, have to be interpreted carefully. Bearing this warning in mind, we can still try to detect certain trends and patterns in crime and criminal behaviour, and we can come to some tentative conclusions.

The most obvious trend is that *crime figures* are rising in the United Kingdom. This is not just a British problem; it is common to Western industrial society. A few years ago an FBI report stated that crime in the USA was increasing at four times the rate of population increase, and that

Table 37
Indictable offences: age groups of persons found guilty or cautioned, England and Wales

	Per 100 000 population in each sex and age group						
	1951	1961	1966	1969 adjusted[1]	1969 actual	1970	1971
Persons found guilty							
Males aged:							
Under 14[2]	1503	1425	1622	1522	1560	1467	1177
14 and under 17	2044	2535	3199	3735	4252	4484	4184
17 and under 21	1164	2275	2944	4092	4721	5102	5231
21 and under 30	938	1377	1867	2181	2322	2420	2366
30 and over	301	300	385	480	487	532	550
All ages	645	818	1039	1248	1349	1423	1414
Females aged							
Under 14[2]	119	142	194	187	188	177	118
14 and under 17	195	310	516	501	516	557	512
17 and under 21	160	265	318	456	469	544	617
21 and under 30	104	152	209	296	299	324	346
30 and over	55	72	93	115	115	121	131
All ages	79	111	150	185	187	201	210
Persons cautioned by the police							
Males aged:							
Under 14[2]	376	560	841	1282	1302	1494	1859
14 and under 17	262	410	627	1101	1188	1422	1964
17 and under 21	56	133	166	227	232	242	271
21 and under 30	22	37	44 } 25 }		55	56	63
30 and over	10	10	14 }		17	18	22
All ages	68	104	120	185	192	221	293
Females aged:							
Under 14[2]	47[4]	95	187	275	276	350	472
14 and under 17	38	89	198	293	296	364	576
17 and under 21	16	22	26	38	39	41	40
21 and under 30	9	12	16 } 17 }		19	23	22
30 and over	5	6	11 }		17	18	20
All ages	12	21	33	47	48	57	79

1 For purposes of comparison with earlier years, the total 1969 figures have been adjusted by subtracting the numbers who were found guilty, as a principal offence, of taking a motor vehicle without authority but who were not at the same time found guilty of any other indictable offence.
2 The age of criminal responsibility was raised from eight to ten years on 1 February 1964. This should be borne in mind when making comparisons between years for the 'under 14' age group.
3 Persons to whom written or oral cautions were given by, or under the instructions of, senior police officers as an alternative to taking proceedings in court.
4 1956 figures.
[Source: *Social Trends*, no. 3 1972 (HMSO)]

four serious crimes were being committed every minute. We have not reached that stage, and perhaps we never will, but a number of people have been worried by the rise reflected in the Tables shown in this chapter.

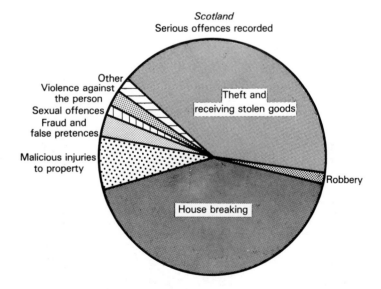

Crime: types of offence known to the police, 1977
[Source: *Social Trends* no. 9, 1979 (HMSO)]

Table 38
Offences against property: analysis by value and age of offender, 1971, England and Wales

	Burglary		Going equipped for stealing	Robbery	Thefts or unauthorised taking			Fraud	Handling stolen goods
	In dwellings	Else-where			Motor vehicles	Shop-lifting	Others[1]		
Offences known to police—total	204·6	237·7				119·3	613·1		
By value stolen:									
nil	35·5	55·3				1·1	19·1		
under £1	10·5	19·0				52·2	90·7		
£1 and under £5	27·9	35·5				40·9	130·2		
£5 and under £10	26·8	24·5				11·1	97·2		
£10 and under £100	78·5	75·3				13·1	240·1		
£100 and over	25·4	28·0				0·9	35·7		
Persons found guilty—total	20·3	42·1	3·0	3·0	28·0	44·3	99·4	13·1	21·9
By sex:									
males	19·3	41·3	3·0	2·9	27·4	21·2	88·5	11·1	19·4
females	1·0	0·8	—	0·1	0·6	23·1	10·9	2·0	2·4
By age:									
under 14	2·7	5·8	0·1	0·2	0·7	2·4	5·6	0·1	1·1
14 and under 17	5·6	9·9	0·5	0·7	6·9	4·7	12·9	0·4	2·8
17 and under 21	5·3	11·3	1·1	0·9	12·3	6·3	24·5	2·2	4·4
21 and over	6·8	15·2	1·3	1·2	8·1	30·8	56·3	10·3	13·6

1 Includes persons found guilty of theft of pedal cycles but the value of such thefts are not recorded and are therefore excluded from the value of stolen property.
[Source: *Social Trends* no. 3, 1972 (HMSO)]

Table 39
Indictable offence: age groups and types of offences, 1971. England and Wales

	Age groups					
	All ages	Under 14	14 and under 17	17 and under 21	21 and under 30	30 and over
Number found guilty of indictable offences:						
All persons	321 836	19 694	49 161	79 304	86 247	87 430
Females	44 528	1 712	5 102	8 109	10 859	18 746
Males	277 308	17 982	44 059	71 195	75 195	68 684
Percentage of males found guilty of:						
Murder or manslaughter	0·1	—	—	0·1	0·1	0·1
Wounding or assault	8·6	1·8	6·6	9·1	10·5	9·1
Other offences of violence	0·2	0·11	—	0·2	0·3	0·4
Sexual offences	2·4	0·6	1·4	1·6	2·3	4·5
Burglary or robbery	24·0	47·1	36·5	25·4	20·6	12·2
Theft or unauthorised taking	49·4	41·5	47·3	52·3	48·1	51·3
Handling stolen goods	7·0	5·6	5·5	5·4	7·5	9·5
Fraud	4·0	0·6	0·7	2·5	5·3	7·0
Other indictable offences	4·3	2·7	2·0	3·4	5·2	5·9
All indictable offences	100·0	100·0	100·0	100·0	100·0	100·0

[Source: *Social Trends* no. 3, 1972 (HMSO)]

Another consistent pattern, not only in the United Kingdom but all over the world, is the breakdown of crime statistics according to sex. In the United Kingdom, men are much more prone to crime than women, and young males are much more prone to crime than young females (or older males). In those societies where male and female roles are more segregated (and where 'a woman's place is in the home') it is less likely that women will be criminally inclined: to put this into technical language, there is a positive correlation between female emancipation and female criminality (see Table 37).

In the UK, women and girls are still much less likely than males to commit offences of any kind, but the figures for females have also tended to rise with the emancipation of women. There are also significant differences in the *kind* of offences committed – girls tend to concentrate on such crimes as shop-lifting, rather than burglary and crimes of violence (see Table 38).

Age differences are also consistently important; the group of people most likely to commit offences are the young males, but the type of offence each age group is likely to commit can be seen from Table 39.

Sociologists are often concerned to explain these patterns of behaviour, as well as describe them. What sort of explanations can be offered? A difference exists here between psychological and sociological explanations: psychologists tend to explain behaviour, including delinquent behaviour, in terms of individual states of mind – they might, for example, suggest that a girl takes to shoplifting because she had an insecure childhood and now feels unloved etc. Sociologists, on the other hand, are more interested in broader social explanations – although they may be just as interested in individuals as individuals.

Sociologists, then, try to explain patterns of behaviour affecting groups of individuals – such as why males are more delinquent than females; why the young more than the old; and, most difficult of all, why is there crime or delinquency at all? There are many different kinds of explanation, and none of them can explain all kinds of delinquency in a completely satisfactory way.

1 Functionalist Explanations

The functionalist view of society tends to be that society is like a machine which has to work smoothly: individuals are like the cogs in a watch – they have to 'fit' in with others. Pieces (individuals) which do not fit in are simply badly made (imperfectly socialised) and have to be made to fit. Up to a point this is a useful analogy, but it breaks down for several reasons. First, a machine does not change (except by getting older and less efficient), but societies do change – many of us think that some changes will actually improve society. Secondly, human are not just cogs in a machine: they make decisions – they h power to decide yes or no. The functionalist view of society delinquency) has therefore been criticised for being 'mech that is, thinking of human beings without considering the sciousness. To see criminals as 'imperfectly socialised' or 'badly brought up' has a grain of truth in it, but it begs a number of questions, as we shall see below when considering deviance.

2 The Delinquent-Sub-Culture Explanation

This view relies on the statistical evidence which tends to show that crime is more common in certain areas than in others. In particular, the slum districts of urban areas are particularly prone to delinquent behaviour. Why? One view is that in such areas community life is breaking down: there may be a rapid turnover of population, many of the people are strangers to each other, living in very poor housing, and including a large number of society's failures or misfits.

In such an area, it might be argued, young people grow up not accepting the usual rules of society: stealing, for example, may be socially acceptable – it is getting caught that is wrong!

3 Relative Deprivation

One criticism of the delinquent-sub-culture explanation is that by no means *all* crime takes place in slums: in recent years there has been a rise in crime – especially juvenile crime – in much more prosperous suburbs. An explanation of this is that you do not have to be starving, or even poor, to feel 'deprived'. One of the characteristics of our kind of consumer society is that shops are full of attractive goods which we are urged to purchase, and advertisements tell us about the desirability of all sorts of expensive items – clothes, records, record-players, motor-cycles, etc. Most people cannot afford to buy everything they would like to, and young people are especially vulnerable – their 'wants' are great, their income limited. If temptation is high and the risk not too great, there may be a tendency to resort to illegal methods of getting what they want.

4 Alienation

The relative-deprivation explanation also seems to make sense, but it could be said that young people (or older people) would not give way to temptation if they had strong feelings about it being very wrong to steal or to be violent. It is often suggested in newspapers, for example, that crime has gone up because youngsters are less religious. This is also probably an over-simplification: people do not have to be religious to obey the rules of society, but it does help if *for some reason* they feel that the rules are good or fair or simply 'ought to be obeyed'. For reasons which I have outlined earlier, it seems to be true that *some* young people simply do not accept the rule-system of society; it may be that the rule-system is so complicated that they do not understand it, or it may be because they just feel that they do not want to be part of that way of life. The hippies in the USA are one example of a deliberate opting out from adult values, and it is suggested that many young people have similar feelings of 'alienation' from society but in a less extreme form.

These are just four of the ways in which sociologists have tried to explain delinquency. There are other theories, but none of them can explain delinquency in a completely satisfactory way. A general weakness of sociological explanations of delinquency is that they often seem to be deterministic – 'we are depraved because we are deprived' (*West Side Story*) – as though the individuals have no *choice* in the matter. Some of the above theories are much worse in this respect than others. Two factors should be stressed. The first is that statistics show *trends*; for example, that working-class boys *tend* to become more delinquent than middle-class boys, or that boys are more likely to be delinquent than girls: this does *not* mean that all boys are delinquent and no girls are! But the figures are often interpreted in that way – that is, there is a serious danger of over-generalising. The second factor is that statistics may show a strong relationship between, say, broken homes and delinquent children, but this does not give a total explanation: We can never say that any example of delinquent behaviour was *caused* by an unhappy home background, as though the individual was powerless in the grip of his environment – there is a very important difference between a statistical correlation and the over-simplified cause-and-effect explanation.

Conformity and Deviance

Another way of looking at this whole question is not to ask 'why delinquency?', but to ask 'why conformity?' It may be a much more important sociological task to explain order in society rather than some aspects of disorder. It seems to be true from anthropologists' studies of other kinds of societies, as well as sociologists' knowledge of industrial society, that all social groups make rules which are enforced by sanctions of various kinds. The rules define, for the members of the group, what must be regarded as 'good behaviour' and what is 'bad behaviour'. If an individual continually breaks the rules of the group, he is treated with suspicion and hostility by the other members of the group: they may insist on his leaving the group (in the past, exile was a more common punishment than it is now), or they may treat him as an outsider although still physically present (the trade-union practice of 'sending a worker to Coventry'), or they may punish him physically. Societies also tend to have a grading system of rules, that is, some rules are more important than others. A person who deliberately avoids paying for a television licence or who evades income tax is regarded by others in our society somewhat differently from a person who steals £15 from the Post Office; adults who are inclined to get intoxicated by drinking whisky are in England regarded with more tolerance than someone taking drugs.

One of the points made by sociologists and anthropologists is that the rules differ from place to place, so they tend to regard rules not as *absolutes* but in a *relative* way. Some would say, therefore, that rules are just customs, historical accidents – that 'morality is geographical'. Up to a point this is true, but it is also true that on major questions of good and evil there is a remarkable amount of agreement: all societies, for example, regard murder of other members of the group as evil, and co-operation as good. The Christian doctrine of 'love your neighbour' is very widespread, although there are plenty of arguments about who counts as a neighbour (and it is easier to decide in small rural communities than in large urban centres). It is possible to draw up a list of general principles which seem to apply to most societies, although there will still be a variety of local rules. The general principles would include, for example:

1 ideas about justice (i.e. what is fair or unfair),
2 respect for other people (e.g. that violence is to be avoided),
3 consideration of others' interests (i.e. that selfish behaviour is undesirable).

Such principles as these are so basic to human life that it is very doubtful whether a society would survive without them. Much less important for survival are rules or customs about diet (what can be eaten and when) or sexual behaviour, or rules about clothing. These rules are really much less important, but they are more easily understood, and people who break the rules may be treated with great hostility, even though someone from outside the group might consider the offence a trivial one.

When talking of deviants or non-conformists, it is important to consider the *kind* of rule which is being broken: is it a high-level general principle of human behaviour, or a local custom which would be quite different elsewhere.

In modern industrial societies the situation is further complicated because, unlike in most simple societies, there is no general agreement about all rules. For example, in the United Kingdom today, people belong to a large number of relgious denominations which disagree about some rules; moreover, many regional or social-class sub-cultures do not have rule-systems which are entirely the same as that of the dominant rule-system in society as a whole. Thus it is possible to be a conformist in one group but to be branded as a deviant in others.

The American sociologist Becker, in a book called *Outsiders*, has classified kinds of deviance in a simple way as follows:

Types of Behaviour	Obedient behaviour	Rule-breaking behaviour
Regarded as deviant	falsely accused	pure deviant
Not regarded as deviant	conforming	secret deviant

According to this simple classification there are four types of behaviour: in two groups (on the left side of the box) the people concerned are obedient to rules; the 'conforming' group are straight-forward non-deviant, obedient members, but the group labelled as 'falsely accused' are those who are regarded as deviant even though their behaviour is completely innocent – they have been 'framed' or are the victims of a 'bum rap'. The danger here is that, having been *labelled* as deviants, they are more likely to behave in a deviant way.

On the right-hand side of the box there is, at the top, the straight-forward rule-breaking deviant, and at the bottom the rule-breaker who is never caught – the secret deviant (many alcoholics and sexual perverts would fit into this category).

What makes people break rules and become deviants? The most simple form of deviant behaviour might be due to ignorance of the rules. Beyond this simple level we have to deal with persons who 'choose' to be deviant; whereas psychological theories tend to see deviance in terms of early childhood behaviour, such as 'damaged personalities', sociological theories tend to look for causes of breakdown or strain in the social system. But what is deviance? There are many different kinds of definition: there is, for example, a statistical definition which assumes a correspondence between 'normal' and 'the average'. By this definition very fat people are deviant, so are the highly sexed or the very highly intelligent. This view has certain advantages, but it gets a long way away from common sense. Another common view is that deviance is something like a disease: just as we talk of a diseased liver when it is not functioning properly, so we might talk of a diseased, pathological, or deviant human being when he is not functioning normally in a group. The difficulty here is that there is much more general agreement about healthy and unhealthy livers than about normal and deviant behaviour. We have already seen that to some extent deviance varies from place to place, but diseased livers are always diseased – that is, the methods of deciding on disease are more *objective* than views about human behaviour.

A more useful definition of deviance is to think of the deviant simply as a rule-breaker (bearing in mind the system of classification on p. 165), irrespective of whether the rule is generally accepted or not; thus behaviour which may be deviant in one group will be perfectly conformist in another.

Belief-Systems

Deviance can only be understood sociologically if it is seen in the context of a *belief-system* of some kind. All societies have beliefs as part of their culture, transmitted from one generation to the next; and when there is a set of inter-connected beliefs, sociologists tend to refer to it as a 'belief-system'. A good example of this would be sets of religious beliefs: Christians, for example, who believe that Christ was a manifestation of an all-powerful god, also have to hold many other connected beliefs. Part of the history of Western society is that many people have developed a stronger attachment to the belief-system of science rather than that of religion. This does not mean, however, that religion does not continue to be a powerful influence in modern society.

One of the essential features of religion is that it involves belief in the supernatural – that is, that *not* everything can be explained in logical, scientific terms. Religion may be seen as an attempt, in pre-scientific society, to explain the world to curious human beings who like to 'know', to have 'answers'. But, even in modern industrial society, religion may be seen as 'functional' – that is, useful for holding society together in some way and keeping it working smoothly.'(Neither of these views, of course, says anything at all about the 'truth' or otherwise of religious beliefs.)

The Social Functions of Religion

The first important function claimed for religion is that a shared system of beliefs and values helps to bind members of a group together and reinforce group solidarity by emphasising the difference between insiders and outsiders (believers and non-believers). This was an important feature of pre-reformation Europe, but, since the break-up of the Catholic church into many denominations and sects, religion often divides societies rather than exerting an effect of solidarity – Northern Ireland is but one example.

Another important function which is claimed for religion is that it sustains the moral order in society. It might be argued that fear of eternal damnation in Hell should be a powerful way of deterring people from immoral behaviour; on the other hand, the evidence to support this is rather shaky. During the Middle Ages, when Christian beliefs were very strong throughout the population, there was no shortage of murder, rape, and robbery. Even today there is no convincing data to support the view that Christians are significantly more moral or less criminal than non-Christians.

A third function of religion in our society is a community one. In the past, the church served as a useful focal point for the whole community – it was concerned not only with religious services but with local and national news, music and drama, and other community festivals. Churches no longer act in this way for the majority of urban communities, although traces of this important function remain in some rural parishes. It is sometimes argued that one of the reasons for the unsatisfactory community organisation of some new towns is that there is no meaningful centre to the community fulfilling just those needs mentioned in connection with parish churches. One of the early French sociologists, Durkheim, who was not a Christian, feared that the decline of Christianity would be accompanied by a general anomie or 'normlessness' in society – that is, by a society which did not know what the rules were! It may be that we have reached the stage of rejecting some of the rules of Christianity without developing a completely rational set of rules for a secular society.

Questions for Discussion and/or Written Work

I

a) What do sociologists mean by 'urbanisation'? Why are they interested in this process?

b) What are the main advantages and disadvantages of urban life compared with living in a rural community?

c) What do sociologists mean by 'community'? Why is community often said to be lacking in large towns and cities?

d) Why is there usually a higher crime rate in towns than in rural areas?

2
'The Growth of Towns.

While few people had much good to say of the towns, no one could deny that they were growing at an amazing rate. Throughout the nineteenth century people were flocking into them in search of work. First of all from the devastated countryside and then in vast numbers from such centres of unemployment as Ireland and Scotland, they came and kept on coming.

By 1851, for the first time in Britain's history, there were more people living in towns than there were living in the country, and the proportion increased as the century wore on. Such a rapid rate of growth was altogether too much for most towns. They were unable to cope.

Local authorities found that drains and sewers and water supplies, just about adequate when their towns were small, were practically useless now that their populations had been doubled or trebled.

Unscrupulous landlords and builders took advantage of the demand for housing. Families were crammed into one small room in buildings containing eight or nine other rooms – and eight or nine other families. When the existing houses in the back streets could hold no more some builders hurried to put up ramshackle, jerry-built shacks that were so insanitary they were a menace to public health.

The Slums

It was not only the houses in the slums that were filthy and disease-ridden. The surrounding streets and alleys were as bad, if not worse. Many of these streets were unpaved, and usually ankle-deep in sewage and other filth. Water was obtained from communal taps often close to open sewers. Long queues formed at these taps and sometimes the supply of water ran out. When this happened water had to be purchased from barrels carried on carts.

The slum areas of the cities were crowded, noisy and dirty. A typical poverty-striken area of Liverpool was declared to be 'the nethermost circle of Hell', and there were many other quarters equally deserving of such condemnation. Penetrating everything in the industrial cities was the dirt-laden air belched out from the factory chimneys. It was impossible to keep anything clean, and the thick, soot and smoke-laden air was responsible for illnesses and death.

Health

In the conditions rampant in these slums disease and death were frequent, if not permanent, visitors.

Lice and vermin flourished in the cramped, overcrowded rooms and houses. Many cellars and other quarters occupied by whole families had no windows, and fresh air was practically unknown. Household filth was tossed carelessly into the streets and allowed to mildew and stagnate. Overflowing cesspits were a common sight. Drinking water was commonly tainted with sewage. Even those who wanted to practice habits of personal hygiene had little opportunity to do so in the slums. Most people did not bother.

As a result epidemics of disease were common. Cholera was a particularly rampant plague and killed thousands of men, women and children. The hospitals were not equipped to deal with epidemics and little could be done for any of the sufferers.

The People

Despite the dreadful conditions, the long hours of work and high mortality rate, the men and women of the slums somehow managed to survive.

They had few pleasures, but one of these was the large number of gin mills and beer shops that abounded in the cities. These fore-runners of public houses provided beer and gin at very low prices and many unfortunate slum-dwellers took solace in this.

Others tried to improve their lot by taking to crime. Stealing and other petty crimes were rife, but punishments for those caught in the act were strict, including transportation or death.

But despite all the temptations to drunkenness or crime, the men and women of the slums usually led decent hard-working lives. Most of them would have given anything to have been able to leave their makeshift homes, but they knew that the chances of doing so were slim.'

[Source: *Poverty* by G. Kent (Batsford)]

a) Why was there so much poverty in England at a time of increasing wealth – i.e. in the mid-nineteenth century?
b) If conditions in towns were so bad in the nineteenth century, why did people leave the countryside to go to live in towns?
c) Why did nineteenth-century governments fail to do anything about poverty in industrial areas?
d) What kind of improvements eventually took place?
e) To what extent are the nineteenth-century problems of urban poverty still with us today?

3 Discuss some of the ideas and theories by which sociologists try to *explain* crime and delinquency. What criticisms would you offer about each of these ideas?

4

For seven months in 1944 the Danish police force was kept under arrest by the German occupation troops. Robberies and larcenies went up dramatically (but crimes such as fraud and embezzlement did not).

In 1919 the Liverpool police went on strike. This was followed by widespread looting.

In 1963 the Home office asked the Government Social Survey to interview a sample of youths aged 15–22 to find out something about their ideas on crime and detection. 808 youths were interviewed. One of the many questions they were asked was: 'If you commited a crime, which of these things would worry you most about being found out by the police?'

	% placing item first
1. What my family would think about it	49
2. The chances of losing my job	22
3. Publicity or shame of having to appear in court	12
4. The punishment I might get	10
5. What my girl friend would think	6
6. Whether I should get fair treatment in court	2
7. What my mates would think	1
8. What might happen to me between being found out and appearing in court	2

[Source: *Crimes, Courts and Figures* by N. Walker (Penguin)]

A Good Experiment

The nearest approach to a sound and successful experiment in testing a deterrent is probably that achieved by R. Schwartz and Sonya D. Orleans, with the help of the United States Internal Revenue Service. Nearly 400 taxpayers were divided into four matched groups. Members of the 'sanction' group were interviewed and asked questions designed to remind them indirectly of the penalties which they might suffer if they tried to evade taxes. Members of the 'conscience' group were interviewed with questions designed to arouse their civic sense and feelings of duty. The third, or 'placebo' group were asked only neutral questions, which avoided both sorts of stimulus. The fourth group were not interviewed at all, in order to test the possibility that even a 'placebo' interview produced some effect (which on the whole it did not seem to do). The interviews took place in the month before the taxpayers were due to file their returns for 1962. Without disclosing information about individuals, the Internal Revenue Service compared the returns of the four groups for the year before the experiment and the year 1962. The reported gross incomes of both the 'sanction' and the 'conscience' groups showed an increase, compared with small *decreases* in the 'placebo' and 'uninterviewed' groups. In other words, the attempts to stimulate both fear of penalties and civic conscience seemed to have had effect.

[Source: *Crimes, Courts and Figures* by N. Walker (Penguin)]

Over a number of years experience has shown that if a man is kept in prison for a long period he begins to deteriorate very seriously. Sir Alexander Paterson doubted whether an average man can serve more than ten continuous years in prison without deterioration. There was no rule in the Home office that a life sentence means release after about ten years, but when the Home Secretary gave figures from time to time it appeared that most cases came into a period of that order. There were occasionally releases after even a year or two, particularly where a mother had killed a child but where the case did not come within the offence of infanticide. There were occasional cases where it was thought that the prisoner was too dangerous to release and he was kept for twenty or more years.

[Source: *Enforcing the Law* by R. M. Jackson (Macmillan)]

Detention Centres

Detention centres nowadays receive more young offenders than either approved schools or borstals. Although, as is true of any penal establishment, the majority of inmates of detention centres have been sent there for thieving, those committed for crimes of violence, traffic violations, and driving away other people's vehicles are found in considerably higher proportions than among the borstal population. A sample of youths aged seventeen to twenty, inmates of detention centres, were studied and interviewed by Dunlop and McCabe. For most of these youths, the energetic, organised pro- gramme, starting at 6.15 a.m., with long periods of closely supervised hard work, and the enforcement of extreme orderliness and clean- liness, with frequent changing of clothes, showers, kit inspections, floor scrubbing, and parades, came as a new experience. Some affected indifference, like the boy who commented. 'It's a lot of shouting, it can't hurt you . . .', but most of them expressed resent- ment at the physical hardship, the prohibition of smoking, and other restrictions. However, a large number seemed to become rapidly tolerant of the routine, and even to enjoy the exercise. Loss of liberty, however, was the one aspect of their punishment which they all felt acutely. In comparison with any delay in their date of release, all other disciplinary measures were felt as minor irritants. . . . Judged by the re-conviction rates of those passing through detention centres (more than a half re-convicted in the three years following release) the system is not particularly successful in deterring future criminality, but then neither are the approved schools and borstals, which give more prominence to reform by education, social training, and indivi- dual attention.

Borstals

The variety of regimes
The English borstals are difficult to describe because they are so varied. Some are run on sternly authoritarian, military-style discipline, others enjoy a comparatively relaxed atmosphere with a great deal of discussion between staff and inmates. Some are built in prison- fortress style and are closed 'security' institutions, others are wide open, with youths working in the surrounding fields or even going out to employment in the neighbourhood. In methods of discipline, in the organization of work and leisure activities, in the use of incentives and grades, and in the amount of personal attention paid to inmates as individuals, borstal governors and housemasters have consider- able scope for initiative. Consequently, what happens in practice, and the impact of the experience upon inmates depends a great deal on the ideas and personality of those in charge. . . . In general, borstals

lay great emphasis on training in habits of steady work, and on trying to arouse interest in a job.
[Sources: *The Young Offender* by D. J. West (Penguin)]

About 63% of borstal boys and 57% of approved school boys are found guilty of further offences within a few years after discharge.
[Source: *Crime in a Changing Society* by H. Jones (Penguin)]

a) Why do some people become criminals?
b) Why do most people conform to the rules?

5

'Many Europeans and Americans use the word 'religion' only when they refer to the three faiths of Christianity, Judaism, and Islam. They are likely to dismiss all other faiths under the heading of 'superstition'. The sociologist finds that this distinction expresses personal prejudice rather than fact. He has learned that all societies in the world have their religions.

The sociologist's aim is to discover that social factors account for the origins and development of a religion, and for the resemblances and differences between one religion and another. This study – comparative religion – is often regarded with suspicion. People think that because the sociologist tries to find out why religions take particular forms, he undoubtedly believes that all religions are false. This is nonsense. Suppose – for purposes of comparison – you were to ask three individuals why they believe the world is round. One might say he had tested the fact by sailing around the earth; another, that his study of astronomy has confirmed the fact; another, that he simply believes what the geography books tell him. You would know exactly why these people have come to believe in the earth's roundness. But would this force you to abandon the belief yourself? Of course not.

Finding the cause of the belief does not destroy its validity. Even when a sociologist finds some rather unsavoury cause for the emergence of a religious belief – say, an era of unscrupulous political agitation – he is not judging the belief itself. He himself may hold any one of a variety of beliefs. Or he may hold none.'

[Source: *Man in Society*, ed. Mary Douglas (Macdonald)]

a) How would you describe sociologists' attitude to religion?

'Religious Membership

It is to a major survey carried out by Social Surveys (Gallup Poll) Ltd for ABC Television in 1964 that we owe the most widely available basic statistics on British religion. The most striking point to arise from this survey was that almost all the adult population of England regarded themselves as belonging to a religious denomination. Only 6 per cent said that they had no religious affiliation, twice as many men as women; 67 per cent classified themselves as members of the Church of England, more than five times the number of Non-conformists (13 per cent) and seven times the number of Roman Catholics (9 per cent); 1 per cent of the population interviewed was Jewish, and 4 per cent belonged to other religions. The Church of England population was equally represented in all the age-groups, but the Nonconformists were strongest in the eldest age-group, the over forty-fives. Roman Catholics, on the other hand, were weakest amongst the elderly: 30 per cent of their members were under twenty-five.

More than four out of five people interviewed (84 per cent) reported that they believed in some kind of god. Only 2 per cent denied categorically that there was a god, the remaining 14 per cent being undecided.

This survey was carried out by Gallup Poll on a sample of 2211 adults aged sixteen and over for ABC Television, and the fact that it was confined to the three television areas of London, the Midlands and the Northern regions, inevitably limits the weight that can be placed on the results.

The following statistics, kindly made available by courtesy of Social Surveys (Gallup Poll) Ltd and the Pastoral Research Centre, are based on an aggregate of 21 495 interviews in 20 quota samples taken in 1963. Unlike the television survey, these surveys were representative of Great Britain as a whole.'

Religious Affiliation in Great Britain 1963

	per cent
Church of England	61
Church of Scotland	8
Nonconformist	11
Roman Catholic	10
Other	4
None	6

[Source: *Religious Institutions* by J. Brothers (Longman)]

'Attendance at a place of worship

According to material collected by Social Surveys (Gallup Poll) Ltd, in 1968, of all those who said they went to church once a month or more, 37 per cent were Church of England, 29 per cent Roman Catholic, 12 per cent Nonconformist, 8 per cent Church of Scotland and 15 per cent members of other denominations.

An interesting breakdown of figures of church attendance was given in the survey carried out for ABC Television published in 1964: 94 per cent of the population considered themselves members of a religious denomination, but only one fifth claimed to go to church on Sundays. But when people were then asked what they did on the previous Sunday, the following picture emerged:

1 Of every 100 members of the Church of England, 13 claimed to go to church most Sundays, although only 7 would in fact do so on an average Sunday.

2 Of every 100 Nonconformists, 30 claimed to go most Sundays, but 20 would go on the average Sunday.

3 Of every 100 Roman Catholics, 59 would claim to go most Sundays, but only 23 would go on the average Sunday.

National "average" statistics of church attendance have to be interpreted cautiously because the influence of religion – or lack of influence – varies very considerably from area to area.'

[Source: *Religious Institutions* by J. Brothers (Longman)]

b) i) Is England a Christian country? Justify and explain your answer.

   ii) What kind of distinction might a sociologist want to make between church membership and participation in religious activities?

   iii) What effect does religion have on behaviour?

Further Reading

Healy, S. *Town Life*. Batsford (Past into Present Series)

Whitaker, B. *Crime and Society*. Blond (Today's History Series)

Jones, H. *Crime in a Changing Society*. Penguin

Brothers, J. *Religious Institutions*. Longman

12
The Political System

The Political System and its Connection with Sociology

It is sometimes suggested that economics is concerned with the resolution of the problem of unlimited wants and limited resources, and that political science is concerned with the study of the value-systems behind the resolution of these problems and also of their enforcement. For example, in our society we have the 'problem' of allocating purchasing power, in the form of money, to individuals most of whom would like more; as in many other societies, some people have to be persuaded to do hard, unpleasant work for comparatively low wages – the methods of persuasion, negotiation, and, if necessary, coercion are all part of the concern of political scientists. Another useful description of politics is that it is the study of power – or how individuals influence and control other individuals. It certainly needs to be stressed that politics is *not* simply concerned with the workings of political parties and government, although this is an important part of the work of political science.

Political science or politics can be a study in its own right – a separate subject – but how the power structure operates in society as a whole and relates to the social structure is clearly the concern of sociologists as well. This chapter will then, be concerned with the study of power in society. Power does not exist on its own: it is part of the structure of relationships between people. Sociologists are particularly interested in the patterning of these relationships: who dominates whom? who has power over whom, and how much? Sociologists are generally reluctant to admit that this might be a random process or just a matter of luck; it is far more likely, for example, that fathers who are 'powerful' would *tend* to have sons who are also 'powerful'. This leads us on to questions like, 'What kind of people are in "power" or are "powerful" in Britain today?'

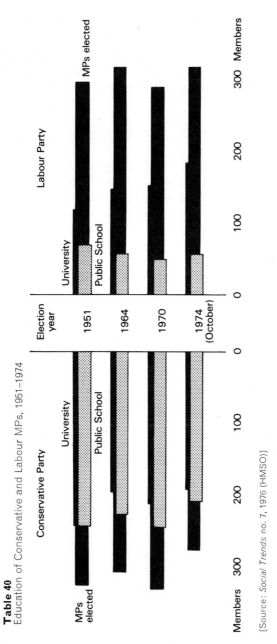

Table 40
Education of Conservative and Labour MPs, 1951–1974

[Source: *Social Trends* no. 7, 1976 (HMSO)]

Table 40 shows interesting educational differences between Labour and Conservative MPs.

In some other countries there may be a number of influential *power groups* (such as the army in some developing countries, or the church in some Roman Catholic countries), but most sociologists would agree that there are two important power structures or elite power groups in the United Kingdom – economic power groups and the political power groups. Some sociologists, with a certain amount of evidence, would say that at the top of these two power pyramids there is a great deal of overlapping: that the governing elite is very closely identified with the economic elite – the property-owning individuals and groups in society. The tendency for the landed gentry and nobility as well as the rich bourgeoisie to continue in power in an increasingly 'democratic' country has puzzled and intrigued many writers.

The following Table maps out the occupational differences between MPs of the three major parties.

Table 41
Occupation, sex and age of MPs, 1974 (UK)

	Labour	Conservative	Liberal	Other	Total
Occupations:					
Barristers, solicitors	43	59	3	3	108
Journalists, publishers, and public relations	28	27	1	2	58
Doctors, surgeons	6	3	—	—	9
Teachers, lecturers	76	8	2	6	92
Farmers, landowners	—	21	2	3	26
Company directors, managers, and other business	62	137	4	8	211
Engineers	29	3	1	—	33
Trade Union officials	19	—	—	—	19
Other non-manual workers	20	5	—	1	26
Manual workers	28	—	—	—	28
Not stated	8	13	—	4	25
of which: men	301	269	13	25	608
women	18	7	—	2	27
Total	319	276	13	27	635
Age groups:					
Under 40	61	63	4	13	141
41–60	203	189	8	12	412
Over 60	55	24	1	2	82
Total	319	276	13	27	635

[Source: *Social Trends* no. 8, 1977 (HMSO)]

The following Table shows the particular importance of a public school background.

Table 42
Percentage of people in various élite jobs educated at Public School (GB)

a) The establishment
 The Civil Service, under-secretary and above (1970) 62
 High court and appeal judges (1971) 80
 Church of England bishops (1971) 67
b) Education
 Vice-Chancellors, principals and professors in
 English and Welsh Universities (1967) 33
 Heads of colleges and professors at Oxford and
 Cambridge (1967) 49
c) Commerce and industry
 Directors of 40 major industrial firms (1971) 68
 Directors of clearing banks (1971) 80
 Directors of major insurance companies (1971) 83
d) Politics
 Conservative Members of Parliament (1970) 64
 Conservative Members of Parliament (1974) 73
 Conservative Cabinet (1970) 78
 Labour Members of Parliament (1970) 8
 Labour Members of Parliament (1974) 9
 Labour Cabinet (1970) 29
(percentage of 14 year olds at school in England
and Wales, 1967 2·6)

[Source: *Social Class Differences in Britain*, by Ivan Reid (Open Books Publishing Limited, 1977)]

In *The New Anatomy of Britain* (1971), Anthony Sampson examined the patterns of relationships in law, business, and the Bank of England, as well as the Conservative party and government. The account is a complicated one, but there is a good deal of evidence to support the idea of inter-connected networks of power and influence, with public schools, Oxford, and Cambridge as important features of the networks.

How has the ruling class managed to survive despite 'democratisation' in the nineteenth and twentieth centuries? There are a number of important historical reasons for the survival of the 'power elite'. The first is that parliamentary reform in the nineteenth century took place gradually and without completely dividing the old aristocracy from the newer capitalist class; for a time the two parties (Tories and Whigs) did represent these two different groups, but they gradually merged into a fairly unified upper-class/middle-class Conservative Party. Thus the ruling elite was able to convince the middle classes that the upper classes were justly and rightfully leaders, and that middle-class interests were not neglected. Similarly, large numbers of the working class, when they eventually got the vote, also identified with 'the old order' rather than with the new Labour Party.

But these are two separate points: the first is that there is a ruling elite with considerable influence over important decision-making procedures; the second, that a large section of working-class voters appear to use their votes in a way which is against their own class interest. The first of these has been examined above. We will now look at the second in more detail. At every general election, the *pattern* of voting according to social class is similar, despite the tendency for 'swings' to occur. A typical study showed the following pattern:

Table 43
Social Class and Voting Behaviour

	Objective social class % voting			
	1, 2, 3	4	5	6, 7
Conservative	66	80	28	17
Labour	23	16	66	80
Liberal	11	4	6	3
Number	52	57	263	237

[Source: *How People Vote* by M. Benny, A. P. Gray, and R. H. Pear (Routledge & Kegan Paul)]

In this sample, 28% of class 5 (mainly skilled manual workers) and 17% of Classes 6 and 7 (semi-skilled and unskilled workers) were declared Conservative voters. If there were not a large proportion of the working classes who vote Conservative, the Labour Party would probably have been in power continuously since the end of the war.

What explanations do sociologists offer for the existence of working-class Conservative voters?

You will have noticed in the Table shown above that voters are broken down into the seven groups of the Hall–Jones classification (see p. 92 for discussion of this scale) according to *objective* social class. This means that they are put into one of the seven categories by a sociologist or research worker according to occupation or husband's occupation. But many people who are 'objectively' working class (i.e. by reason of their job) still think of themselves as middle-class. Such people are referred to by sociologists as 'subjectively middle-class', and they are just as likely to vote Conservative as those who are 'objectively middle-class'. In other words, what you think you are is just as important as what you actually are – probably more important!

Table 44
Social Class and Voting Behaviour

Actual status self-class
% voting

	Above average		Below average	
	'Middle'	'Working'	'Middle'	'Working'
Conservative	75	38	60	17
Labour	14	52	32	80
Liberal	11	10	8	3
Number	101	29	112	417

[Source: Adapted from *How People Vote* by M. Benny, A. P. Gray, and R. H. Pear (Routledge & Kegan Paul)]

We should be careful of looking at this as a simple process of cause and effect, however. It may not be correct to say that some working-class people vote Conservative because they think they are middle-class; it may well be that working-class people who vote Conservative gradually come to think of themselves as middle-class *because* they vote Conservative. The relationship between subjective class and voting behaviour may be a complicated cycle of reinforcements rather than a simple matter of cause and effect.

Another sociological explanation of working-class Conservative voters is the so-called 'deference voter'. This theory suggests that some working-class adults have been socialised into thinking of themselves (and people like themselves) as inferior and incapable of 'ruling'. Such people, according to the theory, would think of aristocrats, or those who had been to public schools, or even managers and businessmen, as *'natural leaders'* who would do a better job of running the country than potential leaders with more humble backgrounds. A detailed study of such thinking is contained in *The Working Class Tories* by E. S. Nordlinger (1967). One Table adapted from this book is shown below (Table 41): working-class voters were asked about the kind of political leaders they would prefer. The Table shows the difference between working-class Tories and Labour supporters in their choice.

Table 45
The Peer's Son *v.* the Clerk's Son as a Political Leader

	Tories	Labour
Peer's son preferred	41	20
Clerk's son preferred	25	47
Both equally good	23	21
Depends on other things	9	8
Don't know	2	3
Total per cent	100	100
Total number	320	127

[Source: Adapted from *The Working Class Tories* by E. S. Nordlinger (MacGibbon and Kee)]

A third possible explanation of working-class Conservative voters, which was popular at one time, was the *affluence* argument. According to this view, the better-paid members of the working classes were becoming more and more 'middle-class' in their life-styles, and part of their middle-class life-style was to vote Conservative. This view is sometimes referred to as the embourgeoisement thesis – the idea that some working-class people were becoming bourgeois or middle-class in their tastes and habits. Some of those who put forward this view stressed that voting behaviour would be especially likely to change in a Conservative direction if the family moved away from a traditional working-class area into a new town or suburb.

This was a fairly popular pseudo-sociological view until some serious research was undertaken by a group of sociologists in the

181

'affluent' car-manufacturing town of Luton (see *The Affluent Workers* by Goldthorpe, Lockwood, Bechhofer, and Platt, 1968). This research showed that, although these workers were among the best-paid manual workers in the country, they showed very little tendency to move to the right in their voting behaviour.

Table 46
Voting for three main parties in general elections, 1955, 1959 and voting intention 1963/64: manual and white-collar samples

	Lab. %	Cons. %	Lib. %	Total	Number
Manual					
General Election 1955	83	15	2	100	157
General Election 1959	80	16	4	100	188
Voting intention 1963/64	79	14	7	100	199
White Collar					
General Election 1955	32	55	13	100	40
General Election 1959	30	55	15	100	47
Voting intention 1963/64	32	58	10	100	50

[Source: *The Affluent Worker: Political Attitudes and Behaviour* by J. H. Goldthorpe, D. Lockwood, F. Bechhofer, and J. Platt (Cambridge University Press)]

Within this study it was found that the most affluent workers in the sample (i.e. the highest paid) tended to be even stronger Labour Party supporters than the others. In general it seemed clear that they were tending to continue to see the Labour Party as a reason for their affluence – that is, as the party which was committed to the policy of better conditions for working people.

Table 47
Reasons for attachment to Labour Party: Manual and White-Collar Samples

Class of reason	Manual (N = 145) Times mentioned	White-collar (N = 13)
General 'working-class' identification with Labour (or against Conservative)	86	4
Favours social and welfare services included in Labour Party programme	19	5
Family tradition	18	3
Better off economically under Labour (or worse off under Conservatives)	16	3
Favours more economic planning and nationalisation	10	2
Labour have men to do the job; approves of Labour men	5	1
Would like to see change; would like to see Labour given a chance	4	2
Really wants to vote Liberal, but no candidate	3	1
Other miscellaneous pro-Labour or anti-Conservative reasons	32	5
All reasons	193	26
No clear reason given, D.K.	13	1

[Source: *The Affluent Worker: Political Attitudes and Behaviour* by J. H. Goldthorpe, D. Lockwood, F. Bechofer, and J. Platt (Cambridge University Press)]

One interpretation of this research is that the embourgeoisement idea was based on a confusion between relatively unimportant aspects of life-style, such as buying cars or furniture, and really deep-rooted commitment to ways of thinking about society and its structure. Much more important than standards of living are the social groups that individuals belong to and how people think of themselves in relation to the rest of society.

A more convincing kind of explanation of voting behaviour has been put forward by Frank Parkin. This theory suggests that all the most important institutions in Britain are essentially conservative. (We should note that 'conservative' in this context does not mean Conservative in the party-political sense, but conservative inasmuch as they *look back* in time, rather than to the future; they tend to want to keep things as they are, rather than encourage change, and so on.) These conservative institutions in our society would certainly include the church, public schools and Oxford and Cambridge universities (and possibly the majority of *all* schools and universities), elite groups in the armed services, the press and other mass media, the monarchy, aristocracy, and the world of finance such as the Bank of England and big business generally. According to Parkin, political choice is one indication of an individual's commitment to a wide range of social values, and the values associated with socialism or the Labour Party are, in a sense, *deviant* values because they conflict with the dominant, conservative values of English society. In any capitalist society the parties of the right have a built-in advantage over those of the left, such as the British Labour Party. Not only does the Labour Party have a 'deviant' image which makes it more difficult to get elected, but once it is 'in power' it has to face the hostility of the conservative establishment which makes it more difficult for the work of government to go on – especially if it has a reforming programme – and which also serves to reinforce the deviant image of the party in the eyes of the electorate. Parkin, therefore, sets himself the task not of explaining the working-class Tory, but why most working-class adults vote in a way which is deviant – that is, vote Labour. His argument is basically that individuals will vote Labour if they belong to groups whose value-systems are in some way anti-capitalist. If they live and work in traditional industrial-working-class sub-cultures they are protected from the dominant, conservative value-system. Those working-class men who work in large factories or in coal mines and who live in working-class estates are likely to vote Labour irrespective of their 'affluence' or high wages.

Parkin is concerned with voting behaviour in Britain as a whole. A point not mentioned by Parkin which I would like to stress is that Parkin's theory would also explain the very important differences within Britain – namely the voting behaviour of the Welsh and Scots, contrasted with the English. Without the Welsh and Scots tendency to vote Labour, the Conservatives would tend to be in power permanently!

I would suggest that, whereas Parkin is correct in suggesting that to vote Labour is deviant behaviour, in the sense of being anti-establishment in *England*, the reverse is true in Wales and Scotland, where there are powerful historical traditions of an anti-English establishment kind. In most of Wales and Scotland the Church of England is *not* influential; universities and schools have a Welsh or Scottish nationalistic bias, rather than a conventional English ethos; both Welsh and Scottish business interests have long resented the dominance of London; and so on.

Parkin's theory would support the view that the mass media, consciously or unconsciously, preserve the status quo – the present state of affairs – that is, a conservative view rather than a Labour Party view, and still less a revolutionary view. But how important are the mass media in shaping our views – in particular our political views?

The Mass Media

It is often suggested that today more and more people are enslaved by ideas put forward by newspapers and television. At the other extreme, it has been suggested that the media have little or no influence on most people – that the media reflect the views of the audience, rather than shape them. What is the evidence?

To start with, we should make a distinction between different kinds of views. There is evidence from market research that certain kinds of advertising campaigns do influence people's buying habits, but this is a long way away from proving that deep-rooted attitudes and values (including political values) are much affected. There was a time in the USA when advertising men claimed they could 'package and present' a presidential candidate in such a way as to make him irresistible to the nation, but these extravagant claims have no supporting evidence.

Not much detailed evidence is available about the political effects of television, but what there is should make us sceptical of the view of the all-powerful media. One piece of research which is easily available for study (in *Media Sociology* by J. Tunstall, 1970, Constable) was undertaken by the University of Leeds Research Unit. Surveys were carried out on the general elections of 1959 and 1964.

The 1959 study was designed to examine the impact on voters of election propaganda. A sample of electors was studied before and after the election campaign, and the general conclusion was that, although there had been a swing to the right, this was not connected with exposure to propaganda. Television viewing did tend to increase electors' knowledge of the political issues but was not responsible for dramatic changes in voting intention. Attitudes did change, but it was *not* possible to connect these changes with viewing (or newspaper reading). The researchers concluded that viewers generally recognise propaganda and resist it as such; when changes did occur it was the result of 'individual judgment'. On the other hand, 'floating voters' were equally protected from the media by apathy and indifference. The general conclusion was that political campaigns serve to reinforce attitudes and intentions, rather than make conversions.

This kind of evidence should certainly make us cautious about accepting the view of the average viewer or reader as completely pliable and at the mercy of the media men. But it was limited to a short time-span, and we know much less about the kind of influence Parkin has suggested – that is, that the media (along with most other institutions) transmit a fundamentally conservative and conformist acceptance of things as they are. To test that kind of theory would need very different research. What we can be fairly sure about is that it is unlikely that political behaviour will be the result of any one isolated event or experience such as as seeing a television programme or reading a newspaper article. Political behaviour, and any other kind of social behaviour, is a complicated process – usually the result of a variety of interrelated social experiences. None of this research supports the view of man as a totally predictable animal, reacting automatically to the environmental stimuli he happens to receive. It looks as though, after all, human beings might have something like free will.

Questions to be Discussed and/or Written Work

I

'The third edition of Webster's New International Dictionary includes among its definitions of political science one which is very different from any appearing previously. According to this definition, political science is "a field of inquiry devoted to an analysis of power in society". Though this idea is new to Webster's, it is not new to American political scientists. The notion that they should focus their attention on power began to appear in the 1920s and slowly gained ground until by the end of World War II it was generally accepted. It carried political scientists from the study of governments into a consideration of how all organizations, from General Motors to the local Baptist Church, "govern" themselves. Not only did the new field of study stretch far beyond the traditional boundaries of political science and invade other social sciences but also many came to feel that it did not form a cohesive whole. For these reasons and others, dissatisfaction with the new definition developed. Actually, the vanguard of political science was beginning to move away from it about the same time Webster's third edition was being published. The remaining definitions of political science in this new edition tend to be either highly experimental or circular. Thus we will doubtless do best to retreat to the first definition given in the second. Political science is "that branch of the social sciences dealing with the organization and government of states".'

[Source: *The Social Sciences*, ed. J. U. Michaelis and A. Montgomery Johnston (Allyn and Bacon)]

a) What do you think would be the best way to describe political science to someone who knew nothing about it?
b) What is the difference between politics and economics?
c) Why are sociologists interested in political behaviour?

2

Table 48

Percentage of Posts Filled by those with a Public School Education

	%
Conservative Cabinet (1964)	87
Judges (1956)	76
Conservative MP's (1964)	76
Ambassadors (1953)	70
Lieutenants General and above (1953)	70
Governors of the Bank of England (1958)	67
Bishops (1953)	66
Chief executives in 100 largest firms (1963)	64
Air Marshals (1953)	60
Civil Servants above assistant secretary (1950)	59
Directors of leading firms (1956)	58
Chairmen of government committees of enquiry (1944–60)	55
Members of Royal Commissions (1960)	51
Civil Servants above and including assistant secretary (1950)	48
All city directors (1958)	47
BBC governors (1949–59)	44
Members of Arts and British councils (1950–59)	41
Labour Cabinet (1964)	35
Top managers of 65 largest firms (1953)	33
Members of government research councils (1950–5)	31
Labour MP's (1964)	15

Members of the Cabinet

Taking all members of the Cabinet from 1868–1916, 68 per cent came from Public Schools. In the period 1916–55, the figure had only fallen to 52 per cent. However this decline is mainly due to the rise of the Labour Party, and not the democratization of either party. Between 1886 and 1916 just over 80 per cent of Conservative Cabinet ministers had been to Public School. Between 1916 and 1955 the average fell to 70 per cent. In 1959 it was 87 per cent. The proportion of Public-School men in Labour Cabinets has also risen. In the 1924 and 1931 governments 17 per cent of the members came from Public Schools. In the new Labour Cabinet, 35 per cent come from Public Schools.

[Source: *Power in Britain*, ed. J. Urry and J. Wakeford (Heinemann Educational)]

a) What is meant by 'the ruling class'?
b) What is the connection between the so-called ruling class and public schools? Why does this connection exist?

c) Why are sociologists interested in the question of a ruling class?

d) If a government wanted to reduce the power of 'the ruling class', what action would it take?

3   Discuss some of the reasons which have been put forward to explain the existence of so many working-class people who vote Conservative. Comment on the evidence which is available.

4   Why does Parkin suggest that conservative values are dominant in English society? To what extent do his views fit in with your own experience?

5

During the General Election of 1959, Joseph Trenaman and Denis McQuail surveyed the political opinions and media exposure of a sample of electors, who were interviewed before and after the campaign. Although they detected a campaign swing of attitudes in favour of the Conservative Party, they reported that the political viewing engaged in by the sampled voters had made no difference at all to the outcome. In the words of Trenaman and McQuail, '. . . political change was neither related to the degree of exposure nor to any particular programme or argument put forward by the parties.' Following the emergence of similar results from a series of surveys in other countries, a veritable law of the political impotence of all the mass media (including the press and radio as well as TV) was eventually formulated. This was supported by an ingenious explanation, which, purported to show why neither floating voters nor more stable electors were persuadable by mass communications.

On the face of it, floating voters – electors who are willing to switch from one party to another – should be open to influence. But because many of them have only a faint interest in politics, they tend to pay but a cursory attention to political affairs through the mass media. Consequently, they were said to be shielded from media influence by their own apathy and indifference. What about the rest of the electorate? When following a campaign, they were said to look mainly for messages emanating from their own favoured candidates and parties. Thus, they were also protected from media influence – by their tendency to engage in what sociologists called 'selective exposure'. Even if they happened to receive propaganda from some alien political source, they would usually interpret it in the light of their existing opinions and loyalties. For all these reasons it was concluded that a political campaign mounted through the mass media usually 'reinforces more than it converts'.

[Source: 'The Political Effects of Television' by Jay G. Blumler, from *The Effects of Television*, ed. James Halloran (Panther)]

a) What is meant by the statement that 'the mass media reinforces more than it converts?

b) How do you reconcile that view with the following:

'In 1938 Orson Welles was responsible for broadcasting as a radio play "The War of the Worlds" which was about an invasion of the earth by Martians in spaceships. The radio play began by announcing the invasion from Mars as if it were a news report; as a result, about a million people apparently believed that there was a real invasion. There was widespread panic, many people leaving their homes in terror.'

[Summarised from *The Invasion from Mars* by H. Cantril (Princeton University Press)]

c) In what ways might Parkin's views (see pages 180–182 above) be relevant to this question?
d) More daily papers are Conservative rather than Labour in their political sympathies.
   i) Why is this?
   ii) Is it important?
e) Why are sociologists interested in the mass media?

Further Reading

Butterworth, E. and Weir, D. *Sociology of Modern Britain.* Fontana. (Chapter 6, articles on 'Power')
Urry, J. and Wakeford, J. (eds) *Power in Britain.* Heinemann Educational Books
Worsley, P. (ed.) *Problems of Modern Society.* Penguin. (Especially Part 4, 'The Politics of Inequality')
McQuail, D. *Towards a Sociology of Mass Communication.* Collier-Macmillan

Glossary

ALIENATION   Alienation means that an individual or group of individuals feel separated from some aspect of their life – especially their work. Sociologists have suggested that in capitalist societies the process of industrialisation has made some kinds of work meaningless and that factory workers, for example, find no satisfaction in their work.

ANOMIE   Normlessness: a social condition where members of a group feel that they do not know what the rules or norms are.

ANTHROPOLOGY   Anthropology may be regarded as one discipline, 'the science of man', or as a collection of disciplines. Since the science of man is very wide, anthropology has often been subdivided into *physical anthropology*, which deals with the biological development of man and his evolution and *social anthropology*, which deals with the principles of human relations in all societies, but especially in simple or pre-industrial societies. There are clear connections between social anthropology and sociology.

ASSOCIATION   A number of individuals who interact with each other for a specific and limited purpose. An association of people is held together by clear rules, rather than by personal relationships; 'association' is thus very different from 'community'. A trade union or a pressure group such as the Noise Abatement Society might be examples of associations.
'Association' can also be used as a process; i.e. to be in association with someone means to be connected with them for a specific, limited purpose.

AUTOMATION   Industrial processes which use machinery and computers not only to make the goods but also to control the rate of production, the input of materials, and the co-ordination of the whole process.

BOURGEOIS, THE BOURGEOISIE Originally these were French words referring to the middle class of French citizens, especially free-men of a burgh. In France these were distinguishable in law from peasants and also from the 'gentlemen'. Marx used the word in a more general sense to mean those people in industrial societies who owned wealth or capital, rather than being gentle-men land-owners. Marx predicted that the bourgeoisie would become the dominant group and thus be in conflict with the workers or proletariat.

BUREAUCRACY In everyday speech, 'bureaucracy' is often used as a term of abuse or criticism about the 'red tape' of the Civil Service or other large organisations. As used by sociologists, 'bureaucracy' is not a term of abuse: it simply describes certain characteristics of our industrial society (which some sociologists such as Max Weber have seen as advantages). The essential characteristics of a bureaucratic large-scale organisation are:
1 specialisation of roles (workers tend to become experts);
2 there is a system of rules which everyone has to obey (no exceptions made for the boss's son, etc.);
3 there is a hierarchy, and people are promoted up the hierarchy according to recognised skills (very often by examinations, diplomas, etc.);
4 a bureaucratic organisation is impersonal in the sense that rules are clear and exceptions are rarely made (it is a 'rational' system where everyone knows the rules and sees them to be fair).
It has often been pointed out that, in practice, bureaucratic organisations may be quite different from the above description (some have suggested, for example, that organisations only work by bending the rules in an intelligent way).

CAPITAL That kind of wealth which can be used to produce more wealth, i.e. either money, or plant such as a factory, or stocks and shares, etc.

CAPITALISM 'Capitalism' is used to refer to those industrial societies with the following characteristics:
1 the means of production (i.e. ownership of money, factories, etc.) is in the hands of private individuals, rather than the State;
2 trade operates in a reasonably free market (i.e. with few government controls), and profits are made as a result of this trading;
3 workers sell their labour on the same market principle, i.e.

they work for those who pay the highest wages;

4 the profit motive is supposed to stimulate economic activity and keep the system going.

CASTE The most rigid form of social stratification. Individuals born into a particular caste stay there for the whole of their life. The caste system is very often reinforced by religious beliefs, so that it is said to be the will of god that some have greater power, wealth, and prestige than others. This is the case in the Hindu caste system.

CENSUS A government survey, normally held every ten years, to collect accurate information about the size and distribution of the population. This information and other details are collected by means of a questionnaire.

COMMUNE A group of people living and working together, especially in modern China. The word is also used for groups of people in the West who opt out of the usual way of life and live together and develop their own way of life.

COMMUNITY A group of people within a society; smaller, less self-sufficient and in closer contact with each other than the society as a whole. Sometimes 'community' is used to refer to a group of people living in a particular place. 'Community' is often contrasted with 'association', community being a much closer network of personal relations.

CONFORMITY To 'conform' is to obey the rules, conventions, or norms of a social group. Most groups demand some degree of conformity. An individual who obeys automatically all the rules might be said to be a 'conformist'.

CONTROL GROUP In some kinds of experiment, comparisons are made between subjects (i.e. people or animals) who have received special treatment and those who have not. In a medical experiment, a treatment group or experimental group might be given a new drug; a very similar group of people (the control group) would not take the drug. At the end of the experiment both groups would be examined to see if there were any differences.

CORRELATION A measure of the degree of association between two variables. Where there is no relationship at all between two variables, the correlation coefficient is 0 (zero). When there is a perfect correlation the coefficient will be $+1$ in the case of a positive correlation and -1 in the case of a negative correlation.

Perfect correlations are rare, and most correlation coefficients referred to might be about +0·8 (high correlation) or +0·3 (low correlation). For example, there is a positive correlation (for obvious reasons) between height and weight (i.e. tall people tend to be heavier than short people), but the correlation is not perfect because there are some short fat people and some very tall thin people. The correlation might be +0·6. Similarly there is a positive correlation between children from broken homes and delinquency, but it is a fairly low one – i.e. there are plenty of normal children from broken homes and plenty of delinquent children from 'stable' families.

CULTURE Everything in a society that is learned and passed on to the next generation. Those aspects of human behaviour which are transmitted socially rather than genetically. A major difference between human beings and other animals is that most behaviour is the result of culture (which has been learned) rather than instinct (which has been acquired genetically).

DEFERENCE VOTER One category of working-class Tories; those working-class individuals who are said to vote Conservative because they feel that the Conservative Party represents the upper class who are the natural leaders of society.

DELINQUENCY Socially disapproved behaviour (not necessarily crime). 'Juvenile delinquency' means socially disapproved behaviour of young people.

DEMOGRAPHY The scientific study of human populations, especially their size, structure, and development.

DEVIANT 'Not normal' in the sense of breaking the rules or norms of a group.

DIVISION OF LABOUR Specialisation of roles, either in society as a whole or within a factory or other work situation. See also *industrialisation*.

EGALITARIAN Someone who believes in a greater degree of equality or social justice in society. Often contrasted with *elitist*. The word is also used as an adjective, for example, egalitarian policies.

ELITE A fairly small group of individuals in a society who exercise a good deal of influence and control over that society. An elite may be an elite by birth (e.g. the English nobility up to the beginning of the nineteenth century, and probably later) or the elite may be a 'money' elite who have power because they have wealth (according to Marx, the capitalist class or bourgeoisie since the nineteenth century). Reference is also sometimes made to an 'academic' elite, i.e. those people who have achieved influence in society because they have achieved high educational qualifications.

ELITIST   An 'elitist' is one who believes that it is very important for an elite to be preserved and encouraged in education, etc.

EMIGRATION   Movement of individuals out of a country to take up permanent residence in another country.

ENTREPRENEUR   A business man or contractor or 'middle man'. An 'entrepreneur' does not earn a living by making anything himself, nor even necessarily by interest from capital. An entrepreneur makes a profit by seeing what demands exist or might exist and by arranging for those demands to be satisfied.

ETHNIC GROUP   Sociologists tend to dislike the word 'race' unless it is used very precisely and in a limited way to refer to major groupings such as the negro race, the caucasian or white race, etc. It is quite wrong to talk of 'the English race' or 'the Jewish race'. On the other hand, it is useful to be able to refer to groups smaller than these major distinctions, and for this purpose the term 'ethnic group' is used. Ethnic groups have cultural and perhaps some physical characteristics in common.

EXPECTATION OF LIFE   A useful indication of the general health of a country can be obtained from the calculation of the expectation of life. In 1841 a new-born boy could be expected to live on average until he was forty, by 1971 he could be expected to live until he was sixty-eight. These are average figures, and the difference in life expectation is not so much caused by the old living longer as by the fact that fewer babies die now. In other words, the fact that in 1841 the expectation of life for males was only forty years does not mean that there were only a few people aged sixty or seventy years; the average expectation of life was lower then mainly because more babies died at a very early age, and this obviously brought down the average figure. Expectation of life is an average figure from the time of birth (unless otherwise stated in the statistics).

EXPERIMENT   A controlled situation designed to test a hypothesis. See p. 4 for examples.

EXTENDED FAMILY   An extended family includes a married couple and their children, plus the third generation (either grandparents or grandchildren and their nuclear families).

FECUNDITY   See *fertility*.

FERTILITY   The *actual* number of children produced by a woman or group of women. Fertility should be distinguished from fecundity, which means the reproductive capacity of a woman or group of women, i.e. the estimated number of children they *could* produce.

FEUDAL SYSTEM   In the feudal system the relationship between a vassal (an inferior) and his lord (or superior) was based on the idea of a fief. The fief was usually land, but it could be some other kind of privilege. The inferior, when he accepted the privilege or land, became the vassal of his feudal superior and had to swear an oath of loyalty to him. He was obliged to be available for military service and to generally support his lord. While the vassal lived, he was regarded as the *tenant* of the lord.

FLOATING VOTER   Most adults are 'loyal' to one particular political party and either vote for that party in an election or abstain. A minority of voters, however, do not have a fixed commitment of this kind, and these are said to be 'floating voters'. They may vote Labour at one election, Liberal at the next, and then switch to the Conservative Party.

FUNCTION   This term has been taken over from biology and means the contribution of a part of an organisation to the activity of the whole. Some sociologists are critical of the use of the term in sociology because social groups are much more complicated than physical or mechanical activities. It makes sense to talk about the function of the mainspring in a watch or the kidneys in a rabbit, but does it make sense to talk of the function of education or class in our society? When we talk about the 'functions of the family in our society' we are really expressing a view that society could not work if the family did not exist – or would work less efficiently. If the term 'function' is used, we should remember that social life is very complex. Sociologists who rely on the concept 'function' to explain the workings of society are referred to as *'functionalists'*.

GENETIC   The physical characteristics which we acquire from our parents are transmitted by means of genes in the chromosomes. These qualities, which cannot be altered by the environment, are referred to as 'genetic'. Genetic differences are often contrasted with environmental differences. Each individual is, for example, born with a maximum potential height; this is genetically determined, but whether or not the individual reaches that height will depend on environmental factors such as adequate food.

HIERARCHY   A set of groups of people with different amounts of power or control over other individuals and groups. The further up the hierarchy an individual is, the more power he has over those beneath him. The army is a good example of a hierarchical organisation, with a large number of private soldiers at the bottom and a few generals at the top, with other officers and NCO's in between.

HYPOTHESIS   A clear statement which can be tested in some way and then shown to be 'right', 'wrong', or still doubtful enough to need more evidence.

HYPOTHETICO-DEDUCTIVE REASONING   The form of reasoning used by Western scientists. For an idea to be scientific it has to be expressed clearly as a hypothesis or statement which can be tested. A hypothesis can be supported (but not proved) by evidence or can be refuted by evidence, in which case the scientist has to find an alternative hypothesis. Hypothetico-deductive reasoning is an important aspect of scientific method. An idea is not scientific unless it can be tested in some way.

IMMIGRATION   Movement of individuals born elsewhere *into* a country for permanent settlement.

INDUSTRIALISATION   England in the second half of the eighteenth century and the beginning of the nineteenth century gradually ceased to be a society in which most people were employed in farming. Instead, more and more people were employed in manufacturing goods of various kinds in factories. This process, which took place very gradually, is sometimes referred to as 'the Industrial Revolution'. In fact the process of industrialisation went on for a very long time.

INFANT-MORTALITY RATE   The infant-mortality rate tells us how many out of every 1000 new-born babies die before reaching their first birthday. In official statistics, the infant-mortality rate is always expressed for the whole year in terms of 1000 live births.

INNATE Inborn. Those qualities or characteristics that we are born with. The word 'innate' is usually contrasted with 'environmental'; for example, colour of skin is an innate characteristic.

INTELLIGENCE QUOTIENT (IQ) Scores in intelligence tests are sometimes expressed as IQ. This is based on the idea of mental age. The average IQ is 100, so a score of less than 100 is an indication of below-average intelligence, and a score of more than 100 indicates above-average intelligence.

$$\frac{\text{MA (mental age)}}{\text{CA (chronological age)}} \times 100 = \text{IQ}$$

So if a boy aged ten had a score equal to the average 12-year old, his IQ would be 120, calculated as follows:

$$\frac{\text{MA}}{\text{CA}} \times 100 = \text{IQ}$$

$$\frac{12}{10} \times 100 = 120$$

KIBBUTZ A kind of commune which has been developed in Israel. Most kibbutzim are agricultural, and the people work together as a community rather than for private profit. Children are brought up together and spend much less time with their parents than is usual in most societies.

KINSHIP The network of relationships based on 'blood' or marriage regarded as important in a particular society. Primary kin are an individual's parents, brothers, and sisters, plus the individual's own children.
Secondary kin would include the primary kin of all those included above, i.e. father's father, mother's sister, brother's daughter, etc.

MASS MEDIA Means of communicating with large numbers of people (usually one-way communication). Mass media include books, magazines, newspapers, radio, films, and television. (Advertising is sometimes included as one of the mass media, but this is not correct: advertising is simply one use made of the various media – it cannot be included as a medium in its own right.)

MECHANISATION The process by which jobs, very often of a skilled craft nature (e.g. the hand-loom weavers), were replaced by machinery. Skilled workers became redundant and could be replaced by unskilled machine-minders.

MECHANISTIC   Explanations which treat human beings as though they were no more than bits of machinery are often condemned as 'mechanistic'. Mechanistic explanations often give the impression that individuals have no power of choice or free will.

MOBILITY   This word really means 'the ability to move', and sometimes 'mobility' is used in a simple geographical sense, i.e. someone is mobile if he was born in Glasgow but moves to London to work. When sociologists talk of mobility, they usually mean social mobility, and that is the capacity for changing from one social class to another. In our society, social mobility is often connected with education.

NORM   All groups have standards or values which guide their behaviour and determine what is acceptable or unacceptable. The word 'norm' is a fairly wide general term covering official rules such as laws and also informal rules which we might call customs.

Another slightly different use of 'norm' is to indicate what actually happens rather than what is expected (for example, according to the law the speed limit along a certain stretch of road might be 30 m.p.h., but the norm might be 40 m.p.h.).

NUCLEAR FAMILY   A nuclear family is a married couple and their children: a two-generation family. Most people belong to two nuclear families – the one that they are born into and the one that they make themselves when they marry and have children.

PARITY OF PRESTIGE (OR OF ESTEEM)   The idea that different kinds of secondary schools – especially grammar and secondary-modern schools – should be different but equal. The idea did not work out in practice because most people after 1944 still regarded grammar schools as the only 'real' secondary schools; many people thought of secondary-modern pupils as failures of the 11+ examination.

PARTICIPANT OBSERVATION   A technique used by anthropologists and sociologists by which the way of life of a group is observed by a research worker who becomes a member of the group he is studying and takes part in their social activities as fully as possible.

PEER GROUP   A group of individuals of roughly the same age.

PRE-LITERATE   A society is said to be 'pre-literate' or 'simple' or 'primitive' if it has not developed a form of writing. It is used as a descriptive term, not conveying the idea of inferiority in any way.

PRIMARY GROUP   The group of people that an individual has face-to-face relations with – i.e. members of the family or of a class in school belonging to the same primary group; however, members of the AA or the Conservative Party are a group but not a primary group.

PROBABILITY   The chance or 'probability' of a tossed coin coming down 'heads' is 1 out of 2; the chance of throwing 6 on a die is 1 out of 6. The probability of a baby in the UK dying within one year of being born is 17 per 1000. This does not tell us anything about the individual children involved. Similarly, it is statistically more likely that middle-class children will go on to university, compared with working-class children; but this fact about statistical probability should not lead us into thinking that all middle-class children go to university but no working-class children do. The chances are different for each group of children, but probability for a group does not mean certainty for an individual.

PROLETARIAT   This word originally meant the lowest social group in ancient Rome. It later came to mean low-class people anywhere. Marx used it to refer to industrial workers and agricultural labourers who had to work for wages because they owned no capital. Marx predicted inevitable conflict between the proletariat and the bourgeoisie.

QUESTIONNAIRE   A structured list of carefully prepared questions. Questionnaires can be used only with people who are sufficiently literate to be able to understand the meaning of the questions and to write intelligible answers. Where this is not the case, the same questions may be given by means of a structured interview where the interviewer records answers either on tape or in writing. All questions must be pre-tested to make sure that they are not ambiguous, i.e. that they are understood in the same way by everyone. Questions must also not be given in such a way as to encourage certain kinds of answers. Some sociologists say that questionnaires can rarely, if ever, meet all of these requirements.

ROLE   A social role is the pattern of behaviour expected from an individual in a specific social position. For example, an individual's role as son is different from his role as an employee, etc. Some sociologists are unhappy about the use or misuse of 'role', as it seems to remove an individual's freedom of choice.

SAMPLING   The collection of information and coming to conclusions about a whole population by examining only a part or sample of that population. A sample may be either a random sample, by which each item or person has an equal chance of being selected, say, every hundredth name on an electoral roll; or a quota sample where the selection is left to the interviewer, provided that specified numbers in each section of the quota are filled (e.g. four in occupational group A, twelve in B, etc.).

SANCTIONS   Any means used by a group to discourage deviant or non-conformist behaviour, i.e. punishments or signs of disapproval in a wide sense.

SOCIAL CLASS   One kind of social stratification or system of dividing people up into ranks or layers. Social class is based partly on wealth or occupation, partly on prestige, and partly on an individual's power or influence. Unlike other kinds of stratification, class is theoretically 'open' – you can go up or down in the system, but it may not be easy to do so.

SOCIAL CONTROL   'Social control' is the term used to indicate how order and stability are maintained within a society. Under the heading of social control, the following might be included: legal, religious, educational, and political institutions. All of these are partly concerned with order and stability in society, i.e. keeping the system going without too much disturbance.

SOCIAL DIFFERENTIATION   Making generalisations about how individuals and groups in society have different roles and occupations with corresponding differences in prestige and power. See also *social stratification* as one kind of social differentiation.

SOCIAL INSTITUTION   In sociology, the word 'institution' does not mean a building or even an organised body of people. A social institution is a pattern of behaviour which has been accepted for a long time by tradition, and standardised so that clear rules or norms have been established. In our society, social class, education, religion, marriage, etc. would be social institutions.

SOCIALISATION   The process by which an individual learns the rules, values, and symbols (e.g. language) of the social groups he belongs to. The main socialising groups are said to be family, peer group, school, and work.

SOCIAL MOBILITY   See *mobility*.

SOCIAL STRATIFICATION   Stratification is a term taken from geology.

Geologists study the different layers or strata of rock formations. In sociology, 'social stratification' refers to the study of the different layers or horizontal divisions in society. In many societies, occupations or groups of occupations are ranked or given different degrees of prestige. The three major kinds of stratification are:

1 the caste system, where movement from one stratum or caste to another is usually impossible – you stay where you are born in the system;

2 the estate system of stratification, where rank is determined by land ownership (the feudal system);

3 social class, where movement from one stratum to another is not only possible but an essential feature of the system, and capital or wealth tends to be more important than land ownership.

See also *social class*.

SOCIAL STRUCTURE   The pattern of social relationships within a society. The idea behind social structure is that certain aspects of society, such as wealth and power, do not happen by chance but are connected with an individual's position in various groups in that society. Related to social structure are other important concepts such as class, status, and kinship.

SOCIETY   When used by sociologists, the word 'society' does not usually mean a group of people such as the RSPCA. In sociology and anthropology, 'society' can be used to refer to people living in one country and sharing the same culture. In small-scale, pre-literate societies it is fairly easy to identify the society by its culture; but in modern, large industrial societies it is sometimes more difficult, and we talk of 'sub-cultures' within the society.

STATUS   A position in society (e.g. son, policeman, judge, etc.). The word is sometimes also used to describe the prestige attached to a position, i.e. how a position is regarded by the other members of that society. Sociologists make a distinction between achieved status and ascribed status. An achieved status is one gained by effort or action of some kind (e.g. bank manager); an ascribed status is one that an individual is born into (e.g. son or daughter). In a social-class system, achieved statuses are said to be more important than ascribed statuses.

TRIPARTITE   After the 1944 Education Act, all children were entitled to free secondary education. At first, many local education authori-

ties had three different kinds of schools, which were supposed
to cater for three different kinds of ability: secondary-grammar
schools for academic children (about 20%), secondary-technical
schools (about 3%), and secondary-modern schools (for the
majority). Gradually this system has given way to comprehensive schools providing (in theory) a single kind of education for
all children.

URBANISATION The word 'urban' is usually contrasted with 'rural';
the urban (town or city) way of life is regarded as very different
from the rural (or country-village) way of life. The process of
urbanisation can mean two things, probably happening at the
same time:
1 the growth of towns and of the proportion of the population
living in towns; and
2 the spread of the urban way of life to the society as a whole.

Index

British Library Cataloguing in Publication Data

Lawton, Denis
    Investigating society. 2nd ed.
    1. Sociology
    I. Title
    301   HM51

    ISBN 0 340 25503 X

First published 1975
Second edition 1980

Printed in Great Britain for
Hodder and Stoughton Educational,
a division of Hodder and Stoughton Ltd,
Mill Road, Dunton Green, Sevenoaks, Kent
by Hazell Watson & Viney Ltd, Aylesbury, Bucks